MUSIC FROM THE TANG COURT

3

MUSIC FROM THE TANG COURT

3

A primary study of the original,
unpublished, Sino-Japanese manuscripts,
together with a survey of relevant historical
sources, both Chinese and Japanese, and
a full critical commentary

by
LAURENCE PICKEN

with

REMBRANDT F. WOLPERT
ALLAN J. MARETT
JONATHAN CONDIT
ELIZABETH J. MARKHAM

and with

YŌKO MITANI, and NOËL J. NICKSON

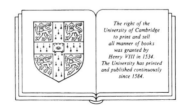

The right of the
University of Cambridge
to print and sell
all manner of books
was granted by
Henry VIII in 1534.
The University has printed
and published continuously
since 1584.

CAMBRIDGE UNIVERSITY PRESS

Cambridge
London   New York   New Rochelle
Melbourne   Sydney

CAMBRIDGE UNIVERSITY PRESS
Cambridge, New York, Melbourne, Madrid, Cape Town, Singapore, São Paulo, Delhi

Cambridge University Press
The Edinburgh Building, Cambridge CB2 8RU, UK

Published in the United States of America by Cambridge University Press, New York

www.cambridge.org
Information on this title: www.cambridge.org/9780521278386

First published 1985
Re-issued in this digitally printed version 2009

A catalogue record for this publication is available from the British Library

Library of Congress Catalogue Card Number: 82-190269

ISBN 978-0-521-27838-6 paperback

To the Memory of
Gustav Haloun
Prince of Teachers

Acknowledgements

A portion of the costs of publication of this fascicle has been
met by grants from the Pei Shan Tang Foundation
北山堂基金 , Hong Kong and from the Hinrichsen Foun-
dation, London. For this generous help, our most grateful
thanks go to the Pei Shan Tang Foundation, as also to the
Hinrichsen Foundation and its Board of Trustees. To Mrs
Niimi Masako 新見政子 we are again indebted for the writing
of a passage in Japanese on p. 6. Research grants from the
Alexander von Humboldt Stiftung and from the Deutsche
Forschungsgemeinschaft are gratefully acknowledged by Dr
E. J. Markham and Dr R. F. Wolpert respectively. Professor
N. J. Nickson gratefully acknowledges the assistance of the
University of Queensland in supporting the work of the Tang
Music Project. For help in matters sinological and japano-
logical we are indebted to Dr D. L. McMullen, Dr Anne M.
Birrell, Mr David W. Hughes, and Miss Nobuko Ishii.

Contents

Glossary of signs

In order to provide the reader with as much information as possible, the transcribed quasi-full-scores also show the Sino-Japanese lexigraphs, etc., used to indicate certain features; by showing these, the reader may have the opportunity to see what the manuscript scores give, as well as our interpretation of what is given.

( )   Round brackets enclose notes etc. to be omitted.

[ ]   Square brackets enclose notes and/or explanatory material editorially supplied.

由   Chinese lexigraph, read *yu* in Sino-Japanese, borrowed as sign for a shake. Where the lute, at the same point, shows a plucked mordent, and the zither a slurred mordent, the mouth-organ shake is presumably to be executed as a matching mordent.

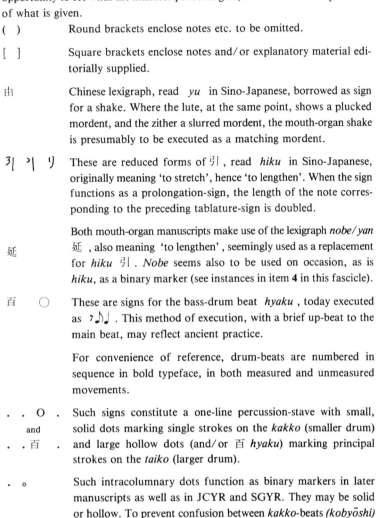   These are reduced forms of 引, read *hiku* in Sino-Japanese, originally meaning 'to stretch', hence 'to lengthen'. When the sign functions as a prolongation-sign, the length of the note corresponding to the preceding tablature-sign is doubled.

延   Both mouth-organ manuscripts make use of the lexigraph *nobe/yan* 延, also meaning 'to lengthen', seemingly used as a replacement for *hiku* 引. *Nobe* seems also to be used on occasion, as is *hiku*, as a binary marker (see instances in item **4** in this fascicle).

百 ○   These are signs for the bass-drum beat *hyaku*, today executed as 𝄽♪𝅘. This method of execution, with a brief up-beat to the main beat, may reflect ancient practice.

For convenience of reference, drum-beats are numbered in sequence in bold typeface, in both measured and unmeasured movements.

. . ○ .
and
. . 百 .   Such signs constitute a one-line percussion-stave with small, solid dots marking single strokes on the *kakko* (smaller drum) and large hollow dots (and/or 百 *hyaku*) marking principal strokes on the *taiko* (larger drum).

. ○   Such intracolumnary dots function as binary markers in later manuscripts as well as in JCYR and SGYR. They may be solid or hollow. To prevent confusion between *kakko*-beats (*kobyōshi*) and binary markers, the latter are shown throughout as hollow dots, regardless of the practice of the individual manuscripts.

丁   This sign, read *tei,* is defined as a short pause in the *Hakuga no fue-fu* (Fascicle 1, pp. 13, 16), but perhaps is to be understood as no more than a break in sound-continuity on the part of the wind, marking the end of an extended phrase or section.

—   This sign, read *ichi*, functions as a binary marker in the earliest manuscripts (Fascicle 1, p. 28), and occasionally appears in JCYR and SGYR also. In transcription the sign is rotated through 90° : |.

火 The lexigraph *ka/huo* 'fire' is a metaphor for speed. In the *Hakuga no fue-fu* (Fascicle 1, p. 9; Marett 1976, 1977) 火 is equated with the lexigraph 急 . This covers a range of meanings, all related to 'swiftly', both in Chinese and in Japanese. When written in sequence following a pitch-sign, the effect of 火 is to halve the duration of the preceding note. Between two pitch-signs, the duration of both notes is halved. In all contexts, the precise significance of 火 is determined by relationships between pitch-signs within a binary unit. Thus, if there are only two such signs within the unit, and if the second is followed by 火 , this note is halved, and the binary unit is completed with a rest. Marett (1977, p. 20) sets out a number of variant uses of 火 — in specifying sequences of quavers in the context of predominantly crotchet movement, for example. ス appears to be used as a speed-writing form of 火 .

二 The numeral '2', written following a pitch-sign, indicates that the note is to be repeated. The duration of the repeated note, and the durations of both notes, depend on relationships between all tablature-signs within the binary unit.

✓ This sign marks a retrograde movement in plucking a string on zither or lute.

Abbreviations

Sino-Japanese manuscript primary sources

CORYF   *Chū Ōga ryūteki yōroku-fu* (c. 1320) Yamanoi no Kagemitsu
HFF   *Hakuga no fue-fu* (966) Minamoto no Hiromasa
JCYR   *Jinchi-yōroku* (c. 1171) Fujiwara no Moronaga
KCF   *Kaichū-fu* (c. 1095) Ōga no Koresue
KF/HSFRK *Ko-fu/Hōshō-fu ryokan* (1201) Toyohara no Toshiaki
RJSF   *Ruijū sō-fu* (eleventh century) Fujiwara no Morozane
RSCY   *Ruisō-chiyō* (c. 1261)
SGYR   *Sango-yōroku* (c. 1171) Fujiwara no Moronaga
SSSTF   *Shinsen shō-teki-fu* (1303)

Chinese and Japanese historical sources

GKMR   *Gakukō mokuroku* (see GKR)
GKR   *Gakkaroku* (1690) Abe no Suenao
JFJ   *Jiaofangji* (c. 756) Cui Lingqin
JGL   *Jiegulu* (c. 848-50) Nan Zho
KKCMJ   *Kokonchomonjū* (1254) Tachibana Narisue
KKS   *Kyōkunshō* (c. 1233) Koma no Chikazane
RMS   *Ryūmeishō* (1133) Ōga no Motomasa
TD   *Tongdian* (801, 803) Du You
TGS   *Taigenshō* (1510-12) Toyohara no Sumiaki
TPGJ   *Taiping guangji* (978) Li Fang
WXTK   *Wenxian tongkao* (c. 1308) Ma Duanlin
WMRJS   *Wamyō-ruijū-shō* (in part, late tenth century) Minamoto Jun
YFSJ   *Yuefu shiji* (Song Dynasty, before 1101) Guo Maoqian
YFZL   *Yuefu zalu* (890-900) Duan Anjie
ZKKS   *Zoku-Kyōkunshō*
ZZTJ   *Zizhi tongjian* (1087) Sima Guang

Introduction

The reader seeking a general introduction to the series, and to the scheme adopted for the organization of the contents of this present fascicle, is referred to the introduction to the first fascicle (1981). There, information will be found relating to the manuscript sources, to problems of transcription, to the development of our 'Tang Music Group' and of our ideas regarding the history of the manuscript tradition in Japan. No attempt will be made here, or in succeeding fascicles, to repeat information once given. Where new manuscript sources come to be used, or where new information requires modification of views previously held, such matters will be recorded in a suitable introduction or postface to a particular fascicle.

As the List of Contents shows, this fascicle includes many more items from the Tang Court repertory than did Fascicles 1 and 2. This necessarily means that the amount of space devoted to an examination of the Chinese sources of information is relatively increased. In this connection, it should perhaps be stressed that, given the vast bulk of the Chinese printed sources, it is impossible that any examination made here should be exhaustive. It is to be hoped that the relatively cursory consideration of those sources here described may stimulate others to a more systematic and comprehensive investigation of literary and historical aspects.

4

Piece :

'A Jade Tree's Rear-Court Blossom'
Gyokuju gotei-ka Yushu houting-hua
玉樹後庭花

Foreword to the piece

Unlike the positions of *Ō-dai hajin-raku, Toraden,* and *Shunnō-den* in the Tang music manuscripts: *Jinchi-yōroku* (JCYR), *Sango-yōroku* (SGYR), *Ruisō-chiyō* (RSCY), and *Ko-fu/Hōshō-fu ryokan* (KF/HSFRK), the position of this piece, following *Shunnō-den*, is certainly not determined by its length fourteen $\frac{4}{2}$ measures only. That position was perhaps determined by its historical associations, and by the fact that it is named almost at the outset in the first of two chapters devoted to *The Refined Music* (*Gagaku/Yayue* 雅樂)in the *Institutes of Tang* (*Tang huiyao* 唐會要, completed in 961). Moreover the piece is mentioned in a context likely to confer on it a certain prestige, albeit of a sinister kind. In the second mouth-organ source here utilized, *Shinsen shō-teki-fu* (SSSTF), however, this piece is in ninth place in the sequence of pieces that follow *Shunnō-den*, and it is preceded by both longer and shorter pieces.

The title and its significance

The translation suggested, 'A jade tree's rear-court blossom', is not how this title later came to be understood, but reflects more closely its original, sixth-century meaning. For an explanation of its earlier significance, I am indebted to Dr Anne Birrell, who has made a particular study of Chinese verse of the Southern Dynasties in the sixth century. The poem of this title which survives (p. 3) fits clearly into the 'Palace-style Poetry' sub-genre of the Southern Dynasties (see Birrell, 1982, pp. 4ff.). She draws my attention (a)

to the frequency with which 'tree' (樹 *shu* or 木 *mu*) is used as a symbol of a wife's immobility in contrast to her travelling husband; (b) to a poem by Xu Fei 徐悱 (d. AD 524) in which a peach-tree in full bloom is an image of a wife's beauty; and (c) to the use of 'jade' (玉 *yu*) as an adjective applied to jewel-like aspects of the person – skin, face, for example. 'A jade-tree', therefore, symbolizes a beautiful woman. 'Rear court' is a reference to the women's part of a house, and in this context to the living quarters of the women of the palace, in apartments opening off the Northern courtyards. 'Rear-court blossom' could be a reference to an imperial concubine or spouse, and the complete title is a metaphor for a beautiful woman, 'blooming' in her appropriate environment.

Although frequently cited in Chinese texts as a single title, *Yushu houting-hua,* it seems probable that there existed songs of differing, but related title; indeed, the *Ci Pu* 詞譜 [1] (1715) refers to 'the Tang Dynasty lyric', *Rear-Court Blossom,* and 'the Song Dynasty lyric', *A Jade Tree's Rear-Court Blossom.* In later centuries (post-sixth century), 'jade tree' [2] could be used as a metaphor for the emperor or for the imperial palace; but, beginning already in the Tang, and fully developed by the latter half of the Ming Dynasty (in the late sixteenth century) – as noted by van Gulik (1961, p. 290) – both terms of this title had

---

1   *Ci Pu* or *Yuzhi* 御製 *Ci Pu* (1715), Taibei, 1964: see pp. 36 and 84.
2   Such trees, with flowers, stems, and leaves, of precious stones or metals – artificial *Bonsai,* as it were – were made formerly as costly *objets de vertu.*

acquired more specific erotic significance, and the title had become improper. There is no evidence that it was felt to be obscene in the sixth century, and a distinction is to be made between the original interpretation and intent of the poem and its later 'perverted' interpretation. (For a glossary of pornographic euphemisms see the study, by Akira Ishihara and Howard Levy (1969), of a section of *The Essence of Medical Prescription,* completed in AD 984.)

History of pieces of this, or related, title

The earliest reference to this piece is probably that in the *Sui History* - the history of the dynasty that reigned from 581 to 617 (*Sui Shu* 隋書), by Wei Zheng 魏徵 - the monographs (*zhi* 志) in which were completed in 656. There it is related that the 'last ruler' of the Chen Dynasty (陳 ; 557-87), Houzhu 後主 , personal name Shubao 叔寶, made[3] this tune (and others) as settings for poems written during convival gatherings that included imperial concubines, scholars, and courtiers.

> When The Last Ruler (Chen Houzhu) succeeded to the throne, he proved to be a drunken sot; when not holding court he spent much time in feasting. Greatly esteeming the pleasures of music, he sent the imperial concubines to practise the flute-[vertical notched flute] and-drum [music] of the Northern region, calling it 'Imitation of the North' or 'Variation on a Northern Style' and when merry with wine [caused them to] play it. For the *Qingyue* [-repertory][4] he also made *Huangli liu,* together with *Yushu houting-hua, Jinchai liang bi* [= *bin*] *chui,* and other pieces.[5] Along with favourite courtiers and others he composed their song-texts. Beauties strove in mutual rivalry in an extreme of frivolity. Men and women sang together. The sound thereof was very sad [*or* 'Their tunes were very sad'].

及後主嗣位，耽荒於酒，視朝之外，多在宴筵。尤重聲樂，遣宮女習北方簫鼓，謂之代北，酒酣則奏之。又於清樂中造黃鸝留及玉樹後庭花，金釵兩臂垂等曲，與幸臣等製其歌詞，綺豔相高，極於輕薄。男女唱和其音甚哀。

Sui Shu, j. 13, *Yinyue* (shang), p. 309
(Zhonghua shuju edn, 1973)

The use of the word *ai* 'sad' calls for comment, since it would appear, at first sight, to be incompatible with the scenes of frivolity hinted at by the text. Nevertheless, the epithet is usually employed in apposition to *le* 樂 'happy', 'joyful'. Conceivably the sound was necessarily *sad* because by Confucian standards improper and indeed sinful in its context.

The Japanese handbook *Kyōkunshō* (*KKS*) (*maki 3*) (Nihon shisō taikei edn, 1973, p. 50) states that the piece is also called 'Golden-Hairpins Droop on Both Shoulders'

---

3 It is prudent not to give to the lexigraph *zao* 造 (to create, to make, to build; to prepare; to institute; to begin from) the meaning of 'to compose'. In the world of Asian music, and of East Asia in particular, it may have meant no more than 'to revise' or 'to arrange' − in the sense of assigning instruments to an ensemble on a particular occasion.

4 Gimm 1966. For *Qingyue* see n. 1, pp. 145-7.

5 See later for more of these titles. See also n. 14 below .

(Kinsa ryō hi sui/ Jinchai liang bi chui 金釵兩臂垂 *).* 'Golden-hairpin' can be a concubine's name; but the text perpetuates a confusion, and the title is probably garbled. This latter title − as can be seen from the preceding translation − is a different piece, also by Chen Houzhu. It occurs in the *Tongdian* 'Current Records' compiled by Du You 杜佑, *c.* 801/803 (j. 145), and a passage from this work is cited in the prefaces to the piece in JCYR, SGYR, and RSCY, This same passage gives four titles of songs attributed to the same author: *Yushu houting-hua, Tangtang, Huangli liu,* and *Jinchai liang bi chui* (these will be translated when the *Tongdian* passage is examined in more detail, p. 8). However, KKS also gives two alternative titles, not so far found in Chinese sources: 'The Jade Tree Piece' (*Gyokuju kyokushi/ Yushu quzi* 玉樹曲子*),* and 'The Chen Palace's Resentment on Seeing Xu Hun's poem' (*Jinkyu en ken Kyo Kon shi/ Chen-gong yuan jian Xu Hun shi* 陳宮怨見許渾詩) This allusion has not been traced but might well refer to critical comment on Chen Houzhu and his principal concubines, in particular on Zhang Lihua 張麗華, often referred to as Zhang Guifei.

The title, both as 'A Jade Tree' and as 'A Jade Tree's Rear-Court Blossom', is listed in the *Jiaofangji* (JFJ, completed 756 or later); but it does not appear in the *Yuefu zalu* (YFZL) of Duan Anjie (*c.* 890) (Gimm 1966). Notwithstanding the extended prefaces to this piece in the vast collectanea of Fujiwara no Moronaga (JCYR, SGYR), no performance of it in Japan is recorded in the *Kokonchomonjū,* nor do the prefaces themselves refer to performances or performers. Nevertheless, the *Ryūmeishō* (RMS) (1133), having referred explicitly to a Chinese performance in 628 (a reference without foundation however − see p. 7) states, as regards the Japanese Court: 'Therefore it is played at the January Court-Banquet' ('Shikareba Shōgatsu Sechie ni kore o sōsu' しかれば正月節會に是を奏す).

An unexplained anomaly is the discrepancy between the length of the piece as stated in the prefaces and RMS, and in KKS. RMS and the prefaces state that, apart from two preliminary measures played in the *Prelude*-manner, the piece consists of twelve measures, and these are repeated eight times; but KKS states that the piece consists of eight Sections (*jō* 帖), the number of measures in each being twelve. The text (KKS) goes on to indicate the positions on the dance-stage (*bu-tai* 舞臺) where successive Sections are to be danced. Since almost all the prefaces (see later, p. 9, in regard to KCF), on the other hand, refer to repeats or times (*hen* 遍 or *hen* 反 = 返), it seems at first sight as if the old Chinese term for a 'time' (*tie* 帖) has been substituted for the more usual forms of *hen.*

However, an upper marginal gloss in a manuscript (in Kyōto University Library) of the *Sango-Chūroku* 三五中錄 makes specific and particular reference to the various Sections, such as reinforces the idea that the piece was at one time a suite consisting of a number of 'movements'. The passage reads: 'According to oral tradition, the sixth Section is called "The Rainbow-Skirt Section"; the seventh Section is called "The Feather-Robe Section" 有口傳六帖

謂之霓裳帖七帖謂之羽衣帖. (The substance of this gloss also appears in KKS.)

This passage is not the only evidence in support of the view that the piece may once have consisted of more than one Section; there is evidence from Chinese sources. The *Ci Pu* (already mentioned) refers (in the commentary) to 'the *Broaching* of "Rear-Court Flower"' 後庭花破子; and the commentary adds: 'regarding the difference between the Tang lyric "Rear-Court Flower" and the Song lyric "A Jade Tree's Rear-Court Blossom"', this was: that that which was called the *Broaching* [in the one] was the *Entering Broaching* [in the other], on account of its many notes' 與唐詞後庭花宋詞玉樹後庭花所謂破子者以其繁聲入破也. Without attempting to explain what that might signify in musical terms, this statement too implies that the piece may once have had a suite-like structure of several movements. It is evident, however, that the *Ci Pu* is referring to pieces of the same, or related title, but of the Tang and Song dynasties, not to the piece by Chen Houzhu. Of the song-texts quoted in *Ci Pu*, none have relevance to Chen Houzhu, and the texts by Mao and Sun in particular, there cited, are not even in regular verse – as is Chen Houzhu's lyric – but are heterometric verse of the type known as *ci* 詞. It would seem that, as so often happened in China, the title evoked resonances that continued to interest poets long after the days of Chen Houzhu. In indicating a possible suite-like structure, the *Ci Pu* referred not to the ruler's song, but to compositions of more or less the same title, popular in succeeding dynasties. This is also implied by the variation in mode and key reported in this same passage, namely, *Xianlu-diao* 仙呂調 (Church Dorian on F) and *Yize-yu* 夷則羽 (also Dorian on F), and *Shuang-diao* 雙調 (Mixolydian on F), if it is assumed that the fundamental of the modal system was C. Since, however, the mode-key *Sōjō* in *Tōgaku* (*Sōjō* = *Shuang-diao*) is Mixolydian on G, it is probable that the Tang fundamental was a tone higher, namely, D. The mode-key of *Yushu houting-hua,* as we have it, is of course (p. 12) Mixolydian on D (Chinese *Yue-diao*).

The fact that the upper marginal gloss in the *Sango-chūroku* equates two Sections of 'Jade Tree' with the suite *Nishang yuyi* 霓裳羽衣 'Rainbow - Skirts and Feather-Robes' – the ballet that made so great an impression on the Tang poet, Bo Juyi 白居易 (Waley 1949), when he witnessed a palace performance in 808 or 809 – is of the greatest interest and importance. Extensive accounts of this ballet-suite survive in the late seventeenth-century *Gagaku*-handbook *Gakkaroku* (GKRK), for example, but no score of any part of this work, in any one of the five tablatures, survives in any manuscript so far seen in Japan. This is the more remarkable since Haku Rakuten, as Bo Juyi (Letian 樂天) is known in Japan, was, and is, so popular a Tang poet for Japanese readers.

That there may indeed have existed some connection between 'Jade Tree' and 'Rainbow-Skirts...' is perhaps also suggested by the list of suites (*daqu*) in the *Jiaofangji*, where the former title immediately precedes that latter.

In the *Gakukō mokuroku* 樂考目錄 'Index of music investigated' (GKR, *maki* 32), 'A Jade Tree' precedes an account of 'Golden-hairpin's two arms hanging down', (better emended to 'Golden hairpins droop on both temples', see n. 14), and this in turn is immediately followed by a lengthy essay on 'Rainbow-Skirts...'. The 'Golden-Hairpin...' entry mentions the tradition (see previously) reported in the *Honpō kyoku-fu* 本邦曲譜 'Musical scores of national pieces' (GKR, *maki* 32), that 'Golden-Hairpin...' as well as 'Rainbow-Skirts...' were different titles for 'A Jade Tree'. GKR also quotes two lines of five monosyllabic Chinese words, ostensibly from the lyric of *Gyokuju gotei-ka,* prefaced by the statement: 'Its words state (其辭曰): "Jade Tree's Rear-Court Flower: The flower may bloom, but will not last for ever" (玉樹後庭花 · 花開不復久)'. This couplet is also cited in the Song 宋 *Yuefu shiji* (YFSJ) 樂府詩集 (j. 47, p. 680 in the Zhonghua shuju edn, Beijing, 1979). The verse-structure, in lines of five syllables, is evidently not that of Chen Houzhu's complete lyric.

Regarding transmission of the piece to Japan, GKR *maki* 31 in the *Honpōgaku-setsu* 本邦樂說 , p. 920, quotes a statement[6] from *Taigenshō* 體源鈔 (TGS) to the effect that it was brought by Fujiwara no Sadatoshi (Fascicle 1, p. 13), and that he himself received the piece from his *piba*/*biwa* teacher, the 85-year-old Lian Chengwu 廉承武 (Wolpert 1977). (Sadatoshi is also credited with the personal importation of the piece next to be examined in this fascicle, *Katen*, p. 20.)

The two-line quotation already translated is said (in YFSJ) to be taken from a lost work, the *Wu Xing zhi* 五行志 *Annals of the Five Elements,* perhaps related to the *Wu Xing dayi* 五行大意 *The General Idea of the Five Elements.* The latter is believed to have been completed about 600, during the Sui Dynasty, and the comment that follows the couplet indicates that, even at that early date, texts relating to the 'jade tree' were given an ominous interpretation: 'Contemporaries felt the song to be prophetic: this was an omen that he would not long survive' 時人以歌讖此其不久兆也.

Chen Houzhu's own lyric (if as such it may be accepted) is at first sight in no way ominous.
Fair sky, fragrant grove, face lofty bower.
Freshly adorned, captivating disposition, apt to topple cities.
Silhouetted against a door-leaf, perfect charm perversely holds back,
Then, leaving the curtain, holds a pose, smiling a welcome.
Bewitching face – as a flower holds dew!
A jade tree in its season lights the rear court.[7]

6 Careful study of the article on *Gyokuju gotei-ka* in the Nihon koten zenshū edn of the *Taigenshō* (3 三本 (下)), pp. 292–303, has not disclosed this statement. It is of interest, however, that *Taigenshō* also quotes the *Huiyao* text with the same variants as the prefaces in the manuscripts.

7 This translation of Chen Houzhu's lyric is based on a literal version made for me by Dr Anne Birrell, 6 November 1981, with suggestions made by Mr Elling Eide in a letter dated 22 June 1982. A translation by Professor J. A. Frodsham is to be found in his book: *An Anthology of Chinese Verse* (Oxford, 1967), p. 198.

麗宇芳林對高閣
新妝豔質本傾城
映戶凝嬌乍不進
出帷含態笑相迎
妖姬臉似花含露
玉樹流光照後庭

Yuefu shiji, di 2 ce, j. 47, pp. 680-1
(Zhonghua shuju edn, 1979)

It was, surely, the licentious extravagance of Chen Houzhu's way of life, and his undignified taking refuge in a well, along with his two favourite concubines, when his palace was attacked (if indeed the incident was not invented), that led to the piece being considered ominously symptomatic of decline. (See, for example, the account of his conduct, downfall, and subsequent protection by Wen-di of Sui, in Wright 1978.)

The most extended discussion of 'A Jade Tree' and its possible influence is that in the *Tang huiyao*, already mentioned (p. 1). The thirty-second chapter of that work as we now have it, in the recension by Wang Pu of 961 (the second year of the Song Dynasty), includes a Section in two parts on 'The Refined Music' *Yayue/Gagaku*' 雅樂上,下.[8] The prefaces to the piece in JCYR, SGYR, RSCY, and the account in KKS, all quote (from the beginning of the section) a continuous passage amounting to 280 lexigraphs.

At six points in this same passage all the citations in the Japanese sources differ from the Chinese text as it now stands, and the possibility exists that these same sources are quoting from an earlier version of the text, perhaps from that presented to the throne in China in 801 – the *Huiyao* of Su Mien 蘇晃. In support of this view, various manuscripts of JCYR, and the account in KKS, head the passage *'Kaiyō/Huiyao'*, while SGYR and RSCY have *'Tō-kaiyō/Tang huiyao'*.(For further discussion, see later, p. 8.)

The content of the passage quoted was evidently of the greatest importance in determining Japanese views on the nature of the borrowed repertory of *Tōgaku*. This becomes particularly clear in the light of an extended paraphrase of the passage (in Heian Japanese) in the earliest of the *Gagaku*-handbooks, RMS (1133). Because of the great significance of this passage, it is proposed to remove the discussion of it from the translation of prefaces to the piece (p. 9.), and to translate it here in its entirety. The Chinese text is given, following the translation. Furthermore, on lines below this text, corresponding to the versions in JCYR (K = Kyōto; P = Palace), SGYR, RSCY, and KKS, are shown lexical differences between the Chinese text of 961 and the Japanese quotations. It is plain that all Japanese sources, regardless of date, are quoting the same version of the text, and this differs from that of the Chinese *Tang huiyao*.

8   Zhonghua shuju edn, in the *Guoxue jiben congshu*, Peking, 1955; see pp. 588, 589. The entire chapter occupies pp. 588-621. Some account of the various recensions of the *Huiyao* ('a classified digest of official documents') will be found in an essay by Professor E.G. Pulleyblank (1960).

Huiyao states: Gaozu [566-635] abdicated [on 3. 9th month. 626; he had reigned from 618-26]. Because he had had to give much attention to military and state affairs, he had not yet had leisure to correct and re-create the *Song-Treasury* [*Yuefu* 樂府]. The old texts of the Sui Dynasty were still used. Not until the tenth day of the first month of the ninth year of Wude [626] did he command the Vice-President of the Court of Imperial Sacrifices, Zu Xiaosun, to put to rights the 'Refined Music'. On the tenth day of the six month of the second year of Zhenguan [628] the music, having been completed, was played. Taizong [= the Emperor] addressed the officials in attendance, saying: With regard to the making of Rites and Music: concerning this the Saints established their teaching by following external things, regarding them as restraining and regulating. How can it be that the rise and fall of good social order stems from this? The Grand Censor, Du Yan, said in reply: The rise and fall of former ages truly derived from music. When Chen was about to perish, there was 'A Jade Tree's Rear-Court Blossom'; when Qi was about to perish, there was the piece 'The Companion'. Passers-by who heard them all grieved with silent tears. This is what is called 'a tune apt to bring about the downfall of a state'. Looked at in this light, it would seem that this was caused by music.

Taizong said: Not so. That musical sounds stir man is a natural principle. Therefore, when those who are happy hear them, they are then pleased; when those who are mournful listen to them, they are then sad. The feelings of sadness and pleasure have their being in man's mind; they are not from music. It is simply that, when a government is about to perish, its people will always be suffering; so they are stirred in their suffering minds and hence, hearing them [= musical sounds] they are, accordingly, saddened. How indeed should the grief and bitterness of musical sounds be able to compel those who are happy to be sad? At present, regarding the pieces: 'A Jade Tree's Rear-Court Blossom' and 'The Companion', their notes are all preserved. If we should cause them to be played for you, we know you would certainly not be saddened.

The Assistant of the Right in the Department of State Affairs, Wei Zheng, approached, saying: The ancients declared:[9] 'Ritual, ritual; Is it no more than presents of jade and silk? Music, music! Is it no more than bells and drums?' Music is located in man's harmony; it is not located in the harmony of notes (*or* in tunes).

The Emperor approved.

高祖受禪。軍國多務。未遑改創樂府。尚用隋氏
①

舊文。武德九年正月十日。始命太常少卿祖孝孫。

JCYR (K)	至	大
JCYR (P)	至	大
SGYR	至	大
RSCY	至	大
KKS	至	大

②
考正雅樂。至貞觀二年六月十日。樂成奏之。

JCYR (K)	☐
JCYR (P)	☐
SGYR	☐
RSCY	☐
KKS	☐

9   The passage is from the *Analects* and is put into the mouth of Confucius himself. See Waley 1938 (1945, 1949), Book XVII, 11, p. 212.

<table>
</table>

太宗謂侍臣曰。禮樂之作。蓋主人緣物設教。以

　　　　　　③　④
為揄節。治之隆替。豈此之由。御史大夫杜淹　對
　　　　　　　　　　　　　　　　　　　　吏

	③	④
JCYR (K)	理	興
JCYR (P)	理治	興
SGYR	理	興
RSCY	理之	興
KKS	□ 理	興

曰。前代興亡。實由於樂。陳之將亡也。為玉樹　王

JCYR (K)	
JCYR (P)	
SGYR	
RSCY	
KKS	

后庭花。齊之將亡也。而為伴侶曲。行路聞之。

莫不悲泣。所謂亡國之音也。以是觀之。蓋樂之

由也。太宗曰。不然。夫音聲感人。自然之道也。

故歡者聞之。則悅。憂者聽之則悲。悲悅之情。

在於人心。非由樂也。將亡之政。其民必苦。
　　　　　　　　　　　　　　　　　　　心告

JCYR (K)	
JCYR (P)	
SGYR	
RSCY	
KKS	

　　　　　　　　⑤
然苦心所感。故聞之則悲耳。豈樂聲哀怨。能使

	⑤	
JCYR (K)	而	然
JCYR (P)	而	
SGYR	而	
RSCY	而	
KKS	而	

　　　　　　　　　　　　　　　　　　⑥
悅者悲乎。今玉樹後庭花。伴侶之曲。其聲俱存。

	⑥
JCYR (K)	具
JCYR (P)	具
SGYR	具
RSCY	具
KKS	具

朕當為公奏之。知公必不悲矣。尚書右丞魏徵

進曰。古人稱禮云禮云。玉帛云乎哉。樂云樂云。

鐘鼓云乎哉。樂在人和。不由音調。上然之。

Since the passage is preceded by the title *Yayue/ Gagaku (Refined Music)*, anyone reading it in isolation might be forgiven for supposing that, no matter how improper the associations of a given piece of music may be, it can have no undesirable effect on listeners, if they are in a suitably wholesome state of mind. Furthermore, since the discussion of 'A Jade Tree's Rear-Court Blossom' follows

a statement that the rectification of *Gagaku* has been completed, and that the rectified music is being played in the imperial presence, it might be supposed that this same piece is part of the *Refined Music* – of *Gagaku*. That this is not so, however, is made abundantly clear by what follows. The account reverts to the actions of Zu Xiaosun in rectifying the *Refined Music* and states first, that 'The *Refined Music* of the Great Tang Dynasty' amounted in all to 32 pieces and 84 systems (*diao* = 'mode-keys' – this latter statement cannot be true since a single piece is likely to have been written in a single mode-key). It then goes on to list the titles of pieces from this repertory that are to be performed at particular sacrifices. None of these items survives in the *Tōgaku* repertory, and there is no evidence that any one of them was ever transmitted to Japan. Surely no further evidence is required that, as late as the reign of Tang Taizong (627-49), the *Refined Music*, in the official Chinese sense, consisted only of pieces linked with imperial sacrifices and court ceremony. The *Refined Music* section of the *Huiyao* has nothing to do with the entertainment music of the Tang Court – with the so-called 'New Refined Music' *Xin Yayue* 新雅樂, the only part of the music of the Chinese Court that reached Japan.

None of the *music* of pieces itemized in the 'Great Tang Refined Music' repertory, as listed in the sequel to this passage from the *Huiyao*, survived in China or elsewhere; but numerous song-texts for pieces with these titles survive in the YFSJ, j. 4-8, for example: 'Contented harmony' *Yuhe* 豫和, 'Great harmony' *Taihe* 太和, 'Awesome harmony' *Suhe* 肅和, 'Expanding harmony' *Shuhe* 舒和, 'Venerable harmony' *Shouhe* 壽和, and others. They are all in regular verse, isometric, in lines of four, five, six, or seven, syllables to the line.

The way in which Japanese readers interpreted the extended quotation from the *Huiyao* is made clear by the paraphrase in RMS which serves as preface to *Gyokuju gotei-ka*. Omitting the opening passage in which the length of the piece, and its repeats, in measures is defined, this preface continues:

> In olden times, this music was ominous. The reason for that was: that [a certain] emperor deigned to like this music. In the course of time, this world becoming absorbed in divination and spirits, the common people were ruined. When the nobles met to investigate the matter, a certain minister said: This music is the cause. [Therefore] they should decide to stop [playing it] for a long time. It was stopped for a long time.
>
> One or two generations passed, and again [a certain] emperor said he felt this music to be excellent; again he was graciously pleased to like it. The nobles [advised him] that this was something that had been stopped because it was ominous. Moreover, they recommended that it should not be played in the imperial presence. [But] the imperial command stated: The music of winds and strings is by no means ominous. The human mind is spontaneously moved [by music]. If one who is heavy-hearted hears it, he is heavy-hearted; if one who is glad hears it, he is glad. It is a thing in accordance with the human mind; it cannot be from music.
>
> Accordingly, on the tenth day of the sixth month, in the second year of Jōgan [that is, the reign-period Zhenguan in the *Huiyao* account], [the Emperor] gave it to the Inner Teaching-

Workshop *Naikyōbō*/ *Nei-Jiaofang* 內教坊 . After the completion of the music, it was played. By that, moreover, the world was not harmed. Therefore it is played at the January Court-Banquet [of the Heian Court].

この樂はむかしいみありき。その
ゆへは、帝王この樂をこのみせさせ
給き。しかるほどに。よにそきれい
をこりて、人民百姓ほろびうせき。
その時公卿せんぎありしに。ひとり
の大臣。この樂の故なり。これをな
がくとどめらるへしとさだめられし
かば。ながくとどめられにき。一兩
代過て。又帝王このがくいみじくお
もしろかりけりとて。またこのませ
給。公卿いみありしかばとどめられ
にし物也。更に〳〵さぶらふべから
ずと申されしに、宣旨云。管絃はき
らにいみなし。人の心を自然に感せ
さする也。なげきある物はきけばな
げく。よろこびあるものはきけばよ
ろこぶ。人の心にしたがふ物也。が
くによるべからず。よりて貞觀二年
六月十日。內敎坊にたまりはりて。
成樂ののちそうす。それによりてさ
らに世らしからず。しかれば正月節
會に是を奏す。

There can be no doubt that this extract from RMS is, to a considerable extent, a paraphrase of the passage from the *Huiyao,* previously translated; but in the Japanese version it has become a parable tending towards a specific end, and its conclusion reveals just what the Japanese chose to accept from the Tang-Chinese original.

It may perhaps be useful to consider the purpose, in the context of Tang China, of the opening passage from the section on *Refined Music* – the music of ritual – in the *Huiyao.* This purpose was to record the historical fact of the 'putting to rights' of the music of Confucian sacrifices and court ceremony; to give a summary list of the sources examined and utilized; to state the titles of music to be used at the various sacrifices. Following this, the section continues with an examination, year by year, of musical matters – repairs to instruments, questions concerning music appropriate to particular occasions, and so on. It must not be supposed that the process of 'putting to rights' involved any examination of entertainment music, since the text tells us precisely what was involved, in a passage that follows on immediately from that already translated.

Prior to this [that is, to the discussion between Taizong and his ministers] Xiaosun, on the grounds that the old [ritual] music of Chen [557-87] and Liang [502-56] [Northern states] mixed up tunes of Wu and Chu [provinces of South-Eastern China], and that the old [ritual] music of [Northern] Zhou [557-81] and [Northern] Qi [550-77] went too far into the empty skills of barbarian tribes, he therefore made a blend of Northern and Southern and, having examined the old tunes [= the old ritual melodies of all the dynasties of the period of division, 420-618], devised The Refined Music of Great Tang.

There follows the list of titles and occasions previously mentioned.

The conversation between Taizong and his ministers takes place, it will be recalled, on the occasion of the first court performance of the revised ritual music. The conversation is an exchange of literary commonplaces, and the emperor initiates the exchange. The concept of the tune able to bring about the downfall of a state goes back at least to the Former Han Dynasty (206 BC to AD 23) and probably to the second century BC. The phrase occurs, for example in the *Grand Preface Daxu* 大序 to the *Mao Shi* 毛詩, the version of *The Book of Songs, Shi Jing* 詩經 , once attributed to Mao Gong among others; and in the *Records of History, Shiji* 史記 of Sima Qian 司馬遷 (145-86 BC), there is an extended account of the terrifying action of several such tunes, memorably translated by van Gulik (1940, pp. 136-8).

In the context of a 'putting in order' of the ritual music, Taizong's comment on the importance attached by 'the Saints' – of whom Confucius was the most exalted – to the making of rites and ritual music, was well chosen and appropriate to the occasion. He asks the reason, not for the concern of the Saints, but for the alleged ennobling or corrupting powers of music. Du Yan's reply is not an original observation, but a statement of a well-known theme of Confucian polemic. What was new in Du Yan's reply was the identification of two popular songs as instances of tunes that had brought about the downfall of states, only two generations or so before the rise to power of the Tang.

Taizong's rejoinder, rejecting the possibility of such music causing such effects, is remarkable at a time when Confucian ideas were being actively promulgated; but it is not an original point of view. The third-century Taoist, philosopher, and outstanding musician, Xi Kang 稽康 (executed for heterodoxy in AD 262), had argued precisely for such a view of the nature of music in a dialogue entitled 'Discussion: that music is without sadness or joy' *Sheng wu ai le lun* 聲無哀樂論 . Parts of the dialogue have been admirably translated by Holzman in an extended essay on Xi Kang's life and thought.[10] The protagonist (who represents Xi Kang himself) is asked, at the outset: 'What are your reasons for contending that there is neither sadness nor happiness in music?' In summary, Xi Kang makes a sharp distinction between that which is the proper sphere of music itself, and that which belongs to the psychology of music. He affirms that music in itself is good or bad, but that it is quite unrelated to sadness or happiness. The passage on the next page strikingly anticipates part of Taizong's argument:

10 Holzman 1957. See pp. 68-72 and passages in Chinese LIX to LXV, pp. 152-5.

The sad mind is concealed within. Meeting with fitting notes, it then manifests [itself in music]. While the fitting notes [in themselves] are unshaped, the sad mind has its governing principle [of sadness]. If the mind governed by sadness then meets with unshaped notes that are fitting, and thereupon manifests [itself in music], this means no more than that it is aware of [its own] sadness.

夫哀心藏于內遇和聲而後發和聲無象而哀心有主夫以有主之哀心因乎無象之和聲而後發其所覺悟唯哀而已[11]

It is, as Holzman puts it, an amoral and non-sentimental view of the nature of music.

The vocabulary of Xi Kang is not that of Taizong; but the parallel character of the thought expressed is evident. A further passage in Xi Kang gives rise to the notion that the discussion with court officials (perhaps aprocryphal) in *Huiyao* was in part stimulated by knowledge of Xi Kang's dialogue on the nature of music: just before the passage quoted, Xi Kang too quotes from the same passage from the *Analects* of Confucius (p. 4) as does Wei Zheng (Waley 1938, Book XVII, 11, p. 212), but Xi Kang follows this with a brilliant, imitative, parallel question of his own devising, making plain the difference between the inner nature of grief and its external signs: '"Music, music! Is it no more than bells and drums?" Grief, grief! Is it no more than weeping?' 樂云樂云鍾鼓云乎哉哀云哀云哭泣乎哉 (j. 5, 1b).

The purpose of Taizong's abrupt contradiction of Du Yan was, presumably, to emphasize the impossibility of moral harm coming to those who were *bien pensant*, no matter what music was heard. 'How should the grief or resentment of musical sounds cause those who are happy to be sad?' But, and let it be repeated, this judgement of Taizong's had no bearing on the repertory of ritual music; it did not justify admission of 'A Jade Tree's Rear-Court Blossom', and 'The Companion' to the *Gagaku/Yayue* repertory.

Consider now what happened to this extract from the *Huiyao* in Ōga no Motomasa's *Ryūmeishō* (RMS). The statement of Du Yan, that 'A Jade Tree's Rear-Court Blossom' led to the downfall of Chen, is given pseudo-historical elaboration in Motomasa's version; but the downfall of Chen was surely due to the fact that Chen Houzhu was a thoroughly incompetent ruler, devoted chiefly to wine, women and song. The text of his lyric (p. 3) is not calculated to corrupt, and is in no way either salacious or ominous. If the song had any particular significance it was as a symptom, rather than a cause, of decadence.

In Motomasa's account, the reason for the song's being ominous was the fact of its being liked by an unspecified emperor. The ruination of the common people was evinced by their preoccupation with practices of divination and

with the spirit-world. This allegation may be an echo of Sui Wen-di's edict against Chen Shubao, in which the reported appearance of malevolent ghosts is urged as a sign of the withdrawal of Heaven's mandate from the Chen ruler (Wright, 1978, p. 141). The proscription of the piece is an invention of Motomasa's. Between the end of Chen and the year 628 (Zhenguan 2), two generations had indeed passed; but *Huiyao* does not make Taizong express pleasure in 'A Jade Tree...'. He merely states his conviction that of itself it could not exert any influence on a mind at ease, free from bitterness.

The imperial command of Motomasa's text is part of the rejoinder put into the mouth of Taizong; the negative in Motomasa's 'by no means ominous' *(sarani iminashi)* is the equivalent of *Huiyao*'s 'not so' *(buran)*. The following: 'The human mind is spontaneously moved [by music]' is in part the equivalent of Taizong's 'That music moves man is a principle of nature' – *shizen* equates with *ziran,* and *kanzesasuru* with *gan.* In the ensuing paraphrase of the *Huiyao* text, Motomasa substitutes *nageki* 歎き for *you* 憂 ; but his *yorokobi* can be rendered in Chinese lexigraphs as two of the terms used by the *Huiyao*: 歡 or 悅び . 'If one who is heavy-hearted hears it, he is heavy-hearted; if one who is glad hears it, he is glad' equates with 聽之則悲 *(kikeba nageku),* 聞之則悅 *(kikeba yorokobu).* His 'it is something in accordance with the human mind' *hito no kokoro ni shitagō mono nari* equates with *Huiyao*'s 在於人心 , but substitutes a more specific word 從ふ *shi-tagau → shitagō* for *zaiyu.* Again Taizong's conclusion: 'They are not from music' 非由樂也 is reflected in Motomasa's *gaku ni yoru bekarazu.*

However, Motomasa again goes far beyond his original when he states that on the tenth day of the sixth month, in the second year of Jōgan (Zhenguan), the emperor (not specified, but 'emperor' is to be understood from the use of the honorific *tamawarite* – from 賜ふ) bestowed the piece on the Inner Teaching-Workshop. The allusion to 'the completion of the music' in Motomasa's account is a misconstruction of the Chinese; what was completed was the revision of the ritual music, and *that* it was which was played. Taizong is indeed made to say that his entourage would not be adversely affected – not caused to grieve – if he should have these pieces played, but there is no implication that they *were* played; and the discussion moves on immediately to further observations on the real nature of ritual and ritual music.

Motomasa's suggestion that it was a matter of observation that the world suffered no harm in consequence of the imagined performance is again a gratuitous elaboration; but his treatment of the entire passage has the advantage that it authorizes performance, in the presence of the Japanese court, of any music whatsoever, including all the kinds of entertainment music borrowed from the Tang Court.

The original passage from the *Huiyao*, and Motomasa's paraphrase and interpretation, are evidently of the greatest importance as determinants of subsequent Japanese

---

11   嵇康集 , edited by Lu Xun 魯迅, j. 5, p.2a, Peking, 1956. The text and *baihua* paraphrase and commentary by Ji Liankang has also been examined:嵇康·聲無哀樂論,吉聯抗譯注, Yinyue Chubanshe, Peking, 1964.

attitudes to the borrowed repertory. Let it be said again: none of that repertory was *Yayue/Gagaku* in the Chinese sense, in the sense in which that term was used in the *Huiyao*, in the sense in which the term was in use at the court of Taizong in 628. A misinterpretation of the Chinese text made possible Japanese acceptance of a popular, vulgar, entertainment repertory, as a music of refinement. In turn, this was a precondition for the transformation of this borrowed repertory into what has indeed become a ritual repertory, one that has functioned for a millennium as an essential aspect of Japanese court ceremonial, a repertory that has evolved its own numinous quality, regardless of its origins.

It may well be asked: How was it that the Japanese missions to the Tang Court never acquired any *Yayue* (*Gagaku*) in the sense of the subject-matter of the *Huiyao* chapter? It is possible that they would not in any case have been permitted to copy the music of Court ceremonial; it is also possible, however, that they were not even permitted to hear it. If indeed they heard it, it is conceivable that they did not find it as attractive as the music of Court entertainment. Whatever Tang ensemble it is that the *Gagaku* orchestra today reflects, it certainly is not the orchestra of Confucian ritual or the 'Drumming & Blowing' bands of military or state processions.

No text of the edition of the *Huiyao* offered to the Throne in 801 survives in Chinese sources; but it is certain that the substance of the passage cited was in existence even before 801, since it occurs, with minor textual variants, in the *Zhenguan zhengyao* 貞觀政要[12] 'Important Governmental Actions in the Zhenguan Period', by Wu Jing 吳兢 who died in 749. Furthermore, two of the six lexical differences (ringed numbers), common to all the Japanese versions of the passage, are occasioned by the necessity of avoiding lexigraphs that had become taboo, because of their use in names of the Tang emperors. ③ 治 is replaced by 理 (note that the Temmei JCYR glosses 理 with 治), because 治 was the personal name of Gaozong 高宗 ; ④ 隆 is replaced by 興 because the personal name of Xuanzong 玄宗 was Longji 隆基 . Clearly the Japanese version was acquired by the Japanese before the end of the Tang Dynasty. Since the last mission during the Tang returned to Japan in 841, it is highly probable that the *Huiyao* quotation is from the first recension, offered to the Throne in 801.

In an attempt to determine when the Japanese first acquired a text of the *Huiyao*, the ninth-century booklist *Nihon-koku kenzai shomokuroku* 日本國見在書目錄 was consulted, but the title *Huiyao* does not occur there. Through the kindness of Mr Yasui Tetsuhiko 安井哲彥 , Executive Secretary of the Japan Academy, the opinion of Professor Sakamoto Tarō 坂本太郎 was sought. The latter very kindly drew attention to the *Tsūken nyūdō zōsho mokuroku* 通憲入道藏書目錄 , the booklist of Fujiwara

no Michinori (Shin-zei 信西) (1106-59) which includes a *Huiyao* in volumes that total 64 *maki/juan* 卷 . The *Tang huiyao* as we now have it amounts to 100 *maki / juan*. It is striking that the work is entitled *Huiyao*, and that the size is less than that of the Song Dynasty *Tang huiyao*. *Either* the copy was defective, *or* this famous twelfth-century soldier, priest, and scholar possessed a copy of the *Huiyao* in its Tang form, so that it may indeed have been possible for Moronaga to have had access to a pre-Song copy.

The *Huiyao/Kaiyō* passage in the prefaces (JCYR, SGYR, RSGY) is preceded by a short extract (50 lexigraphs) from the *Tongdian*.[13] Again there is in all manuscripts a difference of a single lexigraph between the Sino-Japanese version and the Chinese text as now preserved. The passage evidently includes material from the account (in 84 lexigraphs) in the *Sui History*, previously translated (p. 2); but the last sentence perhaps defines the command to He Xu in a manner more in accordance with the legend than with historical fact.

Tongdian states: ' "A Jade Tree's Rear-Court Blossom", "Tangtang", "The Yellow Oriole Perches", "Golden-Hairpins Droop on Both Shoulders"[14] were all items made by Chen Houzhu. Constantly in the company of the imperial concubines, of scholars, and of ministers of the court, he sang together with them and made poems. The Master of music commanded He Xu to choose outstandingly frivolous and voluptuous ones for the making of these pieces.

通典云。玉樹後庭花堂堂黃鸝留金釵兩臂 垂並陳

後主所造恒與宮女學士 朝臣相唱和爲詩大樂 令何

胥 採其尤輕艷者以爲此曲

JCYR		曰
SGYR		曰
RSCY	疋[15]	曰

Tongdian, j. 145,
Section *Za gequ*,
'mixed song-pieces'

13 Du You 杜佑 : *Tong Dian* 通典 *A history of governmental institutions* (see Pulleyblank 1960) presented to the Throne in 801 or 803. See j. 145, Section 'Mixed song-pieces' *Za gequ* 雜歌曲 , Iwen yinshu guan edition, p. 7b. As shown in the display of the Chinese text, following the translation, the prefaces in the Japanese manuscript-tablatures all exhibit one lexical difference from the Chinese text as we have it today; but this difference is not present in the most recent edition of KKS (Nihon shisō taikei, 1973). Again, it is to be supposed that the prefaces have all drawn on the same original.

14 The most recent edition of YFSJ (Zhonghua shuju, Peking, 1979) reads 鬢 *pin* (= hair on the temples), in place of 臂 *bi* (= arm), making much better sense: 'Golden hairpins droop on both temples'.

15 The use of 疋曰 in RSCY suggests that variants in the Sino-Japanese versions may have arisen by dissociation of the name 'Xu' 胥 , separating phonetic and determinative: 疋 , 月 , and with graphic corruption of 月=肉 to 曰 ; with subsequent restoration of 'Xu' in the text. This Sino-Japanese variant might then be read: 'He commanded He Xu, saying: Choose...'

12 See the *variorum* edition of a thirteenth-century manuscript of this work by Harada Tanenari 原田種成 : *Jōgan seiyō teihon* 貞觀政要定本 ; p. 238 (item 189).

Notes on sources in tablature transcribed in this fascicle

Four of the sources used require no introduction, since they were considered in Fascicle 1. These are the two mouth-organ scores, *Ko fu/Hōshō-fu ryo-kan* (KF/HSFRK) and *Shinsen shō-teki-fu* (SSTF), the score for zither, *Jinchi-yōroku* (JCYR), and the score for lute, *Sango-yōroku* (SGYR). In addition to these sources, two new manuscripts of notations in tablature have been made use of. One of these is a reputedly Heian flute-score: *Kaichū-fu* 懷中譜 (KCF) 'Score for the bosom', *or*, written as 懷竹譜 'Score for the bosom -bamboo' (that is, for a flute), said to have been compiled by Ōga no Koresue 大神惟季 (1026-94), but probably of the fourteenth century. The oldest copy recorded is that in the Research Archive for Japanese Music, Uenogakuen College, Tokyo (see Fascicle 1, p. 33), written in 1701 (*Genroku* 元祿 14th year). In addition to a microfilm of that manuscript, we have also used a photocopy of that in the Naikaku Bunko Library 內閣文庫：番號:和 24721；冊:3(1); 函號:199 183; A note on the nature of the system of flute tablature used in this manuscript, and on problems of transcription, will be found on p. 53.

The second newly consulted manuscript is also in flute tablature: *Chū Ōga ryūteki yōroku-fu* 注大家龍笛要錄譜 (CORYF) compiled by Yamanoi no Kagemitsu 山井影光 in the early fourteenth century, probably between 1321 and 1330. The title may be translated as 'The Ōga family's annotated score of essential records for flute' – that is, for the flute of the *Tōgaku* ensemble, the *ryūteki*. Kagemitsu lived from 1273 to 1354 and claimed lineal descent from Ōga no Koresue (and, necessarily, form Ōga no Motomasa also – this fascicle, p. 7). We have used a microfilm of the copy in Tenri University Library (Signature: 761/35/A 668). This is a very early copy, but not the original, the latter is still preserved by descendants.

A comparison of KCF and CORYF shows the two manuscripts to be closely related, with the Tenri copy of CORYF showing some degree of degradation (as compared with KCF) in the care exercised in the writing of the tablature. Even copies of KCF differ among themselves, however, in the degree of clarity with which the original features of the tablature are copied.

Prefaces to the piece from the sources in tablature

KCF

A Jade Tree's Rear-Court Blossom : 14 bass-drum beats; but if repeated use twelve beats. New music. A middle-sized piece. 玉樹後庭花 拍子十四 但有二反用十二拍子 新樂 中曲 When the dancers emerge use a *bongen* 品玄 [a type of standard modal prelude; see Fascicle 2, p. 17; Shiba 1972]; when they retire use a *kanjōshi* 上調子 [see ibid. – another, and lengthier, type of standard modal prelude]. 舞出時用品玄 入時上調子

It is said that there are three quasi-*Preludes:* the opening two [measures of] *Prelude;* at the end of seven Sections, one [measure

of] *Prelude:* at the end of eight Sections, *Prelude;* that is, three quasi-*Preludes.* 有三女序云初二序 七帖終一序 八帖終序 三女序也

It is also said, however: the first two measures are *Prelude.* After the second bass-drum [beat] blow [= play] *gaku-fuku* [see Fascicle 2, p. 00] up to the fourth Section. From the fifth [= fourth] Section's [bass] drum [beats] onwards blow *gaku-fuku* up to the fourth [= fifth] Section. From the fifth Section's seventh drum-beat gradually quickening complete the sixth and seventh Section in *yo-fuku* [= 'playing of our time'] In the seventh Section, after the eleventh drum-beat, play in the *Prelude*-manner up to the eighth Section – this *Prelude*, together with the previous ones makes four.

又云初二拍子序也第二太鼓以後樂吹至四帖也自五帖鼓以後樂吹 至四帖也自五帖第七拍子以後早々成天六七帖於世快七帖第十一拍 子以後序吹至八帖（此序共二以第七也）

The first measure is played in the preludial manner. After it, play in *gaku-fuku*. Playing slowly, namely, add three-times beats; also, at the end, two measures are played in the preludial manner. This is what is called 'three quasi-*Preludes*'. Also in the seventh Section, after the initial measure, especially fast, completing like *Seigaiha*. The twelfth measure is played in the preludial manner. Completing the eighth Section, play the first measure like a *Prelude*. From the second measure, play especially slowly; then add three-times beats. Following the eleventh measure, the final single measure is played in the preludial manner. 頭一拍子序吹也其後樂吹也緩吹天即加三度拍子又末二拍子序 吹也是號三女序又七帖初拍子以後殊早々成天如青海波第十二 拍子序吹成八帖初拍子猶序吹自第二拍子殊緩吹天則加三度拍 子十一拍子以後末一拍子爲序吹

The preface in KCF illustrates at length the description of 'repeats' as 'Sections' previously mentioned (p. 2). It also indicates three (or four) changes to the 'preludial' manner of playing. These are separated from each other by passages in 'music-blowing' *gaku-fuku* (as opposed to '*Prelude*-blowing' *jo-fuku*). Both terms were encountered in Fascicle 2, p. 13, in the KKS definition of the metrical difference between Section 1 and Sections 2 and 3 of the *Prelude* in *Toraden*. The score itself suggests that the preludial passage (and passages) are to be played without strokes on the *kakko*-drum; and it is to be assumed also that the duration of the unit-note (here transcribed as a crotchet/quarter-note) was longer than elsewhere. Furthermore, performance of the piece was diversified by fast playing at certain points, specifically defined, and by the introduction of 'three-times beats' *sando-byōshi* 三度 拍子 in Section 8. This means, presumably, that bass-drum strokes are to be applied on crotchets 1 and 3, as well as on crotchet 5, in the $\frac{4}{2}$ measures. (See Figure 1).

A scribal lapse seems to have changed fourth to fifth and fifth to fourth in the sequential description of Sections.

The reference to the *Tōgaku* piece *Seigaiha/Qinghai-bo* 'Waves of Kokonor' *(Banshiki-chō)* is not understood. Inspection of the textures of flute and string parts suggests that the pace cannot have been faster than *c.* ♩ = 60.

Of at least equal importance is the fact that these flute versions are evidently decorative variations on the less decorated melodic material of the string parts, and the still

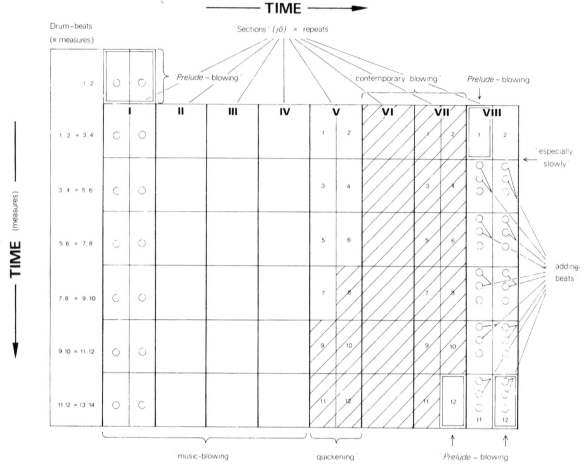

Figure 1   The structure of a performance of *Gyokuju gotei-ka* according to the preface in KCF (see p. 9)¹

less decorated material of the mouth-organ parts. It would not occur to any musician, looking at the flute parts transcribed in this fascicle in relation to the other parts, to regard the flute part as a basic melody, and the string parts and mouth-organ part as reductions of the flute part.

KF/HSFRK

A Jade Tree's Rear-Court Blossom: New music. Eight Sections (*jō* = 条 = 帖). Bass-drum beats of each separate Section, 12; but the first Section has 14.

玉樹後庭花・新樂八条拍子条別十二但初条十四

There is a dance. Emerge and retire to the modal *Prelude*. From the seventh Section onwards beat 'three-times beats' (*sandobyōshi*).

有舞出人調子從七条打三度拍子

SSSTF

Jade Tree: 14 bass-drum beats.
玉樹　　拍子十四

JCYR

　　A Jade Tree's Rear-Court Blossom: drum-beats 14. Should be played eight times; but from the second time onwards the drum-beats [= measures] for each time are twelve. In all, there are 98 drum-beats [2+8×12 measures]. From the seventh time onwards, beat 'three-times beats' [See Fascicle 1, p. 22.]

玉樹後庭¹⁶花拍子十四可彈八反但第二反以後每遍拍子十二 合
拍子九十八從¹⁷第七反打三度拍子

¹⁶Wrongly written in JCYR　¹⁷Abbreviated in original

[Prince]Southern-Palace's Score for *Transverse-Flute* states : 'But by all means, from the end of the sixth repeat add one drum-beat, and this should be struck.' From the seventh repeat it is correct to strike 'three-times beats'. This then is the practice for all pieces. Henceforward in all pieces that permit this, it may be struck. Nowadays in the eighth Section beat 'three-times beats'. When abbreviating, play twice [only]. In the last Section advance the bass-drum.

南宮橫笛譜云但須從六反¹⁸終加一拍子而¹⁹可打也　從²⁰七反²¹
正打三度拍子　此則諸曲通例也　以下諸曲²²准此可打今世第
八帖打三度拍子　略時彈二反終帖上大鼓

Dancers emerge and retire to the *Modal Prelude*. A middlesized piece. New music.

舞出入用調子　　中曲²³　新樂

Both in JCYR and in SGYR an upper marginal gloss over the end of this portion of the preface states: 'The dancers say: When abbreviating, dance the first and the eighth, two Sections [= times].'

舞人曰略時舞第一第八兩帖也

　　From the end of this portion of the preface there follows first: the passage from the *Tongdian* (p. 8); secondly, the passage from the *Huiyao* (pp. 4 to 8).

¹⁸SGYR遍　¹⁹SGYR尚　²⁰Abbreviated　²¹SGYR遍
²²Kyōto MS. inserts 可　²³Ibid. inserts 加

RSCY

The preface to 'A Jade Tree....' in this manuscript differs from that in JCYR at three points only (apart from minor graphic variants): (a) The *Huiyao* quotation is headed *Tang huiyao*, as in SGYR (this Fascicle, p. 4). (b) In the song title, *hua/ka* is written as 華 rather than 花. The former is the older form of the lexigraph and has come to be used with the meaning-extension of 'glory' or 'splendour', perhaps justifying the translation 'blossom', rather than 'flower' in the singular. (c) The quotation from 'a flute-score' parallels that in JCYR from Nangu's *Score for transverse-flute*. It appears then that Ribu-Ō 吏部王 (from whose flute-score the quotation is taken) was another title for Prince Sadayasu (Nangū), and that the *Ryūteki-fu* specified is Nangu's *Score for transverse-flute (Nangū ōtekifu)* of 921.

'A JADE TREE'S REAR-COURT BLOSSOM'

NB: Broken octaves – typical of the more archaic style of zither technique (Fascicle 1, p. 29) – here transcribe complexes consisting of large (higher-pitched) and small (lower-pitched) tablature-signs, not linked by a ligature.

The flute part is given a signature of three sharps, of which two are enclosed in brackets, because we cannot be certain whether the piece was still played in a Mixolydian mode-key or (as the twelfth-century string parts show) in a Lydian mode-key. There can be no doubt that the piece was originally a Mixolydian melody.

The transcription of the flute part (by E.J.M. and R.F.W.) is to be regarded as a first attempt. It is based on the readings of a single manuscript. (A seemingly less florid style is exhibited in the transcription of the flute part of *Ō-dai hajin-raku*, p. 56.) The flute version of 'A Jade Tree's Rear-Court Blossom' shows clearly the relationship between flute decoration and the types of decoration characteristic of the strings. This kind of flute variation on the original *Tōgaku* melody of the mouth-organ part, slowed to a pace such that the crotchet of the transcription occupies an Adagio-Andante common-time bar, but scarcely otherwise modified, constitutes the flute parts of *Tōgaku* performance today.

Displacement of *kakko*-dots (*kobyōshi*) (Fascicle 1, pp. 29, 31) and *taiko*-dots *(hyaku)* from their correct horizontal registration in relation to other tablature signs is frequent in the Naikaku Bunko manuscript used as source for 'A Jade Tree...'. To show both original and corrected positions for both drum beats would have meant making the score too complicated. Accordingly, apart from the indication of a first anticipatory displacement (Fascicle 1, p. 31) in the first measure, neither *kakko*- nor *taiko*-dots are shown.

1 SGYR (right) 一説 'one version states'.
2 JCYR (left) 'up to here preludial lengthening; for the second time and after, in repeating play from this *d – d′*.' 已上序
引.第二反以後 從此一五不［反］彈 . KF/HSFRK also notes 'up to here, *Prelude*' 從此上序
3 SGYR (left) 'up to here preludial lengthening.'

4 SGYR (right) 'for the second time and after, in repeating play from this *d – d'* 第二反以後從此∟也反彈

5 JCYR (right)

6 JCYR: sharpening dot supplied.

7 JCYR: dot supplied yielding mordent in place of ligature.

8 JCYR (left)   'one version states.'

9 SGYR (left)   'one version states.'

14

0 SGYR (right)  'one version states.'

  ᵃKCF: the sign 動 *dō / dong* (Fascicle 1, p. 24) is used by *Hakuga* in defining the execution of 連 *ren/ lian*. Its significance here is not understood. As used in KCF. *ren* seems to mean a rapid, descending sequence of notes. In the transcription this is shown by a zigzag between notes,

  ᵇKCF (left): 'From here perform quickly when doing the fifth time.' 自是早成五帖之時

  ᶜKCF (left): 'When playing one time [only] from here add drumbeats.' 一反時自是加拍子

  ᵈKCF (left): 'When doing three quasi-*Preludes,* from this point blow in the *Prelude*-manner.三女〔如〕序之時自是序吹　Add the beginning of the eighth Section　加初八帖　like one measure in the *Prelude*-manner 猶一拍子序 This time at the end [play] in the *Prelude*-manner, like the beginning 此時終序二如初

Variant version for lute (SGYR)

(1) On the upper stave, the primary version (see Fascicle 1, p. 9), as in the quasi-full-score, pp. 12–15.

(2) On the lower stave, the secondary version ('same piece' *dō-kyoku* 同曲). Though not marked as such, this secondary version is in the melodic style known as *gaku-byōshi* (see Fascicle 1, p. 10).

1 SGYR (left) 'for the second time and after, in repeating play from this *d*.' 第二反以後從此レ反彈

16

Preliminary comments on the structure of the piece

The prefaces, and the accounts in RMS and KKS, make plain that the first two measures serve as a *Prelude* to the twelve that follow. Since the first two are identical with the last two measures of the twelve, the effect is of a refrain repeated nine times, if (as specified) the twelve are repeated eight times.

Since the tune proper – that which is repeated – consists of six musical lines, each of two measures of $\frac{4}{2}$, it may be not unduly fanciful to see a possible relationship between this set of six and the original six lines of Chen Houzhu's lyric. Since the lines of this lyric were each of seven monosyllabic words (p. 4), each line could have been sung to two measures of four crotchets, the last syllable being sung to a minim. This is the common type of musical setting of text-lines of seven lexigraphs in the songs of Jiang Kui of the Song Dynasty (Picken 1966, see p. 131). It may be, then, that twelve measures of $\frac{2}{2}$ have been dilated to twelve $\frac{4}{2}$ measures, as a result of the incorporation of melodic glosses. The possibility of such a dilatation of pieces in the *Tōgaku*-repertory has been evident from the beginning of our studies of that repertory (Picken 1969). In 1969, it was pointed out that, in two instances where the original Chinese text of songs belonging to the *Tōgaku* repertory have been preserved, 'the number of measures in the piece is a simple multiple of the number of lines of seven syllables.' Since that time, Rembrandt Wolpert (unpublished observations) has recorded a number of further examples where the tune that survives in the tablatures is precisely twice the length of that required, if the text is to be sung one note to one syllable.

2   SGYR (left) gloss in flute notation

With six lines of seven lexigraphs, making a total of 42 syllables, Chen Houzhu's lyric is larger than the smaller types of song-text of *c.* 28 syllables (Picken 1966, p. 132), but not as large as the *man* of *c.* 56 syllables (*ibid.*, p. 133). In all probability, then, the piece would have been sung to six musical lines, each consisting of two measures of $\frac{2}{2}$.

Three out of the six lines rhyme, and the presence of a rhyming syllable usually determines the incidence of a drum-stroke. The three rhymes occur at the ends of lines 2, 4, and 6. Their modern pronunciations: *cheng, ying, ting,* rhyme less obviously than their early-medieval forms. In Karlgren's romanizations of archaic, ancient (middle), and modern forms (Karlgren 1957) these are:

818 *e* *ḍïĕng / źïäng / ch'eng
699 *d* *ngïǎng / ngïpng / ying
835 *h* *d'ïĕng / d'ieng / t'ing

all three are today pronounced in the *yinping*, or 'rising' tone of the dialect of Peking, but Karlgren shows 818 *e* and 835 *h* in the even tone, *pingsheng*. From the *Ci-yuan* 詞原 of Zhang Yan 張炎 , it is known that 'a rhyme has a rhyme-beat' (Picken 1966, see fn. 15, 16) and this would seem to define the required musical line as ten measures of four beats (= six crotchets/quarter-notes + one minim/half-note) with drum-strokes on the third and seventh beats of the line.

With so much information already available, it appeared worthwhile to attempt to extract an original song melody, to which Chen Houzhu's lyric might be sung, from the dilated tune. As a first step, the simplest surviving version from among the five parts available – that of the mouth-organs – was reduced to a more-or-less singable compass, inverting the leaps of a minor ninth occasioned by the absence of a $C^\sharp$ in the lower octave of the instrument. The resulting, minimally decorated, melody — much more floridly decorated, however, than any known song melody of the Song or early Yuan periods — is shown as an upper stave in the following illustration. Four of the collaborators, together with Dr D. R. Widdess of the London School of Oriental and African Studies, independently prepared melodies in which each of the two-measure musical lines of the original was reduced to two $\frac{2}{2}$ measures. In the illustration that follows on p. 19, notes with stems (not associated with any stemless note-heads) represent the independent solutions of five different observers. Each stemless note-head adjoining a stemmed note represents a solution not shared with others. The 'number of votes' as it were for a stemmed note is then equal to five *minus* the total of adjoining, stemless note-heads. At one point only does it seem that, on musical and semantic grounds, the minority view makes better musical sense, namely, at the third beat in the first measure of line 2 of the lyric, where *d* on *yan* gives more suitable weight than a repeat of the *b*. Most of the ligatures have been retained from the simplified mouth-organ version of the tune. They serve to give a touch of isorhythm to the first half of each line.

It may be asked whether syllable-melody — that is, 'tone' — played any part in determining the melodic contour of individual musical lines, as it does in the operatic genre *kunqu* 崑曲, for example. That it does not is strongly suggested by the inescapably level pitches to which the rhymes at the ends of lines 4 and 6 are to be sung, notwithstanding the possibly rising character of the syllable-tone. This treatment of two out of the three rhymes encouraged us to ignore, in devising a vocal line, the rising movement in line 5, even though both movements would be appropriate to the tonal accent of the respective final syllables. In the illustration, accents are shown over the transcribed song-text in accordance with the Modern Standard Chinese pronunciation in *Guoyu*.

The chain of fifth and minor third with which the reconstructed vocal line begins is a sequence characteristic of ancient Asian melody, as recognized by Vikár, (see Vikár and Bereczki 1971, p. 52), for example. Only one observer chose to begin the reconstruction on the mediant rather than on the final. As compared with Jiang Kui's song-melodies, the limitation of musical line-finals to dominant and tonic is striking; as shown, one of us suggested endings on the superfinal for lines 3 and 5, but this did not occur to the rest. Even admitting the superfinal, however, the range of cadences at the ends of musical lines is more limited than for any one of Jiang Kui's tunes.

There is no evidence that the Japanese ever received a text for this song, and no evidence that they ever knew an earlier, undecorated version of this melody. It was, conceivably, as an early Tang version, now enshrined in the mouth-organ parts, that they received the piece from China, at latest in 841, and probably not before then, since GKR associates the piece with Fujiwara no Sadatoshi. It may be, then, that we have here an example of embellishment as practised in China, where a popular tune of the sixth

century survived into the early ninth-century entertainment repertory of the Tang Court.

That song-tunes, the size of which is a simple multiple of the number of text-lines in the lyric, are indeed examples of *Chinese* decoration, and expansion, by incorporation of melodic glosses, is made certain where the number of drum-beats *(hyōshi* 拍子 *)* in a piece, *as specified in the earliest Japanese sources,* is a multiple of the number of text-lines. Experience has shown that the number of drum-beats stated in these earliest sources is almost invariably the same as the number of measures observable in performance today. Where small discrepancies occur, these are usually multiples of 2 and may plausibly be linked with the repetition or non-repetition of a given internal phrase or phrases. The constancy of the number of drum-beats implies constancy in the number of measures, and demonstrates convincingly the absolute faithfulness in transmission of the *Tōgaku* tradition, in respect of this dimension, over the centuries, from the earliest times. This use of the number of beats as an important constant in defining a piece, the first item of information to be stated, after the title, had a Chinese precedent (Fascicle 2, p. 100 and n. 14): at least as early as the beginning of the eighth century, this information was recorded, for example, in a Tang-Chinese zither-handbook, in relation to the two movements of the famous battle-suite for 7-stringed zither, *Guangling-san (Prelude & Tune-Proper).*

In summary, we know then that, since the earliest recorded dimensions of 'A Jade Tree's Rear-Court Blossom' are 2 + 12 drum-beats, the piece must have undergone inflation before reaching Japan; and the melodic line preserved in the most conservative of the instrumental parts, that of the mouth-organ, is a specimen of — at latest — Tang-Chinese melodic decoration.

In general then, it may be that, in those instances where inspection shows the length in measures, of pieces for which the Chinese text survives, to be a simple multiple of the number of text-lines, the conservative mouth-organ versions provide specimens of Tang-Chinese melodic embellishment. These in their turn might then provide a basis for comparison with presumably Heian, and post-Heian, Japanese elaboration of string parts, and wind parts other than the mouth-organ. It remains to determine up to what point, both stylistically and in time, Japanese melodic decoration of *Tōgaku* parts was guided by Chinese precedents and, may-be, precepts.

Attention has already been drawn (p. 3) to the variety of mode-keys ascribed to several songs with the title 'A Jade Tree's Rear-Court Blossom'. One is Mixolydian with F as final (if C is the fundamental of the system F G A B^b C D E^b), two are the same mode-key by different names, older and younger: Church Dorian series with F as final; *Yize-yu* and *Xianlu-diao* F G A^b B^b C D E^b. The mediant is natural in the former, flattened in the latter; the subfinal is flattened in both. As we have it in the Sino-Japanese tablatures, the tune is Mixolydian on D. That the Chinese felt the Mixolydian mode-keys to be sad is well attested, and it may be that the concluding sentence of the *Sui History's* note on Chen Houzhu's songs (p. 2); 'The sound thereof was very sad', related to modality. It may be fortuitous, but is nonetheless fact, that the restored tune functions satisfactorily with a minor third between tonic and mediant. Jiang Kui's melodies make plain that the tritone was not avoided during the Song Dynasty, and the sequences: B-A-F (song-lines 4 and 6) in 'minor' versions, would have been perfectly acceptable.

A reconstructed tune for Chen Houzhu's Lyric

5

Suite:
'The Palace of Congratulations'
Katen/Hedian
賀殿

Foreword to the piece

KCF and KF/HSFRK agree with JCYR and SGYR in placing
this piece (*Katen*) next in sequence to 'A Jade Tree's Rear-
Court Blossom'; but in SSSTF, *Katen* immediately follows
'The Singing of Spring Warblers'. In addition to its musical
character, appropriate in tone even to our ears for an
occasion of ceremonial rejoicing, the piece is remarkable in
that, already in the ninth century, and in Japan, it had been
enlarged, by association with two other pieces, to form a
suite (see later). Alone among source manuscripts so far
seen, KF/HSFRK sets out this item in its suite form: first
the *Way-walking* (p. 22) (a kind of *Processional*) which
utilizes the *Quick* of 'The Bird' (p. 30); then the *Broaching*,
probably composed in Japan; next the *Quick* – the piece
Katen proper, reputedly brought back from China by Fujiwara no Sadatoshi in 841; and lastly, as exit-music, a repeat
of the *Quick* of 'The Bird'.

The title and its significance

The title - apparently the name of a building 'The Palace
of Congratulations' - is not known from Chinese
sources. It might be assumed to have designated at least
a hall, if not a palace as such, reserved for Court use on
the occasion of birthdays, new-year's greetings, the presentation of congratulatory presents or other gifts. The title
does not occur in the *Jiaofangji* (JFJ)[1] (see Fascicle 2,

---

1   Tsongshu jicheng edn, 叢書集成 , Shanghai, 1935-40,
     No. 2733, j. 1, pp. 3-5.

pp. 6, 7, 10, 45, 46, 47) in the list of 'Names of Pieces'
Qu-ming 曲名 . There three titles begin with *he* 賀: *He
shengchao* 賀聖朝, *He Huanghua* 賀皇化 , *He shengyue*
賀聖樂 , but none of these seems to be an equivalent of
Hedian. Nor does the title occur in the *Yuefu zalu* (YFZL)
(Fascicle 2, p. 10), or in the *Jiegulu* (JGL) of Nan Zho 南
卓 (848/50).

History of pieces of this, or related, title

The *Wamyō-ruijū-shō* (WMRJS) states:

> Tradition of an older generation relates, ''The Magistrate
> Fujiwara no Sadatoshi, sent to Tang in the Jōwa [reign-period,
> 834-47; the mission extended from 838 to 841], transmitted the
> piece by means of the lute. Hayashi no Sadakura, obedient to
> imperial decree, made this dance.
> 古老傳云承和之唐判官藤原貞敏以琵琶傳曲 林貞倉奉勅作此舞

Since the relevant section of WMRJS only appears in the late
version in 20 *maki* and not in the version in 10 *maki* (and
presumably not in the original in 5 *maki* of which no copy
appears to survive) (see p. 31), it may not be concluded
that this attribution was current already in the tenth century.
Nevertheless, RMS (1133) stresses that it is the *Quick Kyū/Ji*
急 of this music that was transmitted from Tang China and
repeats the association with Sadatoshi, stating that he
learned it on the lute (*biwa/piba*) and returned with it.
According to this source, however, the *Broaching Ha/Po*
破 is also entitled 'Music of Auspicious Omen' *Kashōraku/
Jiaxiang-yue* 嘉祥樂 , and was first used as a *Broaching*
in Japan ('here' *kokoni*). While this might seem to imply

that the piece was devised in Japan, the statement about Sadatoshi's learning it on the lute *follows* these remarks that concern both *Quick* and *Broaching*. This latter title (*Kashōraku*) also does not occur in the Chinese sources. RMS too credits a certain Hayashi with the creation of the dance ('now lost'), but names him Sanekura 直倉 and adds that he was a Chinese ('a man of Song 宋'), presumably Lin Zhencang.

KKS adds further particulars about the circumstances of Sadatoshi's visit to China in the Jōwa reign-period and confirms the association of the piece with him. It also adds the detail that the dance is said to have been devised during the reign of the Emperor Nimmyō 仁明 (833-49). The dance, then, appears to have been built around two unrelated pieces: a *Broaching, Kashōraku*, and a *Quick, Katen*. Furthermore, the *Quick* from the *Bugaku*-piece *Karyōbin* (see later, p. 30) was used as a type of *Processional* (*Michiyuki* 道行) – as stated also in RMS, but there refered to as *Tori*, an alternative title. KKS again (as in the description of *Gyokuju goteika)* uses the term *jō* 帖, where RMS refers only to 'repeats'.

Both KKS and the *Zoku-Kyōkunshō* 續教訓抄 (ZKKS) equate the title *Katen* with an alternative in two different graphic forms: *Gansenraku* 含泉樂 or 甘泉樂 'The Enclosed Spring' or 'The Sweet Spring' (in the Chinese reading *Hanquan-yue* or *Ganquan-yue*); the former title was associated, once at least, with an occasion of congratulation. References to a locality called 'The Sweet Spring' occur already in the *Han History* (*Han Shu* 漢書 – second century AD) in relation to Imperial Progresses[2] undertaken, first, by the Wu-di Emperor (reigned BC 141-87) to 'The Sweet-Spring Palace' in the first month of the year BC 94, and, secondly, by Cheng-di (reigned BC 33-7) to 'Sweet Spring' in the same month of the year BC 13. A poem by the Jian-wen-di 簡文帝 Emperor of the Liang (梁) Dynasty (reigned 549-51 AD), entitled 'Imperial Progress to the Sweet-Spring Palace',[3] seems to be the first poetic allusion to the locality. A further poem, by Liu Xiaowei 劉孝威 refers to 'Avoiding the heat of summer at the Sweet-Spring Palace' 避暑甘泉宮) (YFSJ, p. 1185), but there seems to be no indication in the Chinese sources how a link with 'The Palace of Congratulations' might have existed, or how, at a much later date, this link was made in the thirteenth-century Japanese handbooks. Japanese scholars may well have had knowledge, already during the Song Dynasty, of these poems in the YFSJ; but the title 'Imperial Progress to the Sweet-Spring Palace' also occurs in another Chinese source of the Song period, among a list of '18 pieces of Travelling Music', included under the heading 'Lost melodies: a prefatory essay' (遺聲序論) in 'Music: an abridgement' (樂略), which appears in the vast compilation of 'Current Monographs' (通志) assembled, during the early twelfth century, by Zheng Qiao 鄭樵 .[4]

Japanese scholars may have been acquainted with both these compilations by the end of the twelfth century; but some tradition, as yet undetected, must have been responsible for establishing a link between *Katen* and 'The Sweet-Spring Palace'. It is interesting that Eckardt (1956), without reference to any source, states that there *was* a *Summer* Palace of the Chinese emperors with the title 'The Sweet-Spring Palace', even though the Han emperors seem to have been visiting there in the *First* Month. It is Liu Xiaowei's poem that first implies it was a cool summer retreat. Several localities with the name 'Sweet Spring' are known to Chinese geographers, but that associated with the Wu-di Emperor was the Sweet-Spring Mountain in Shensi Province (陝西) where, originally, a Sweet Spring Palace had been erected with the aid of ghosts and spirits. Wu-di is said to have added to this The Palace Known to Heaven, The Palace of Exalted Brilliance, and The Palace Welcoming the Winds (or, and also, 'of Dalliance'), but, alas, no Palace of Congratulations.

From ZKKS it becomes clear that *Kashōraku* is only a reign-period title, taken from the end of the Emperor Nimmyō's reign, borrowed as title for the piece; and the same source adds most interestingly that it is not uncommon for names of reign-periods to be borrowed for pieces – thus supporting our interpretation of the alternative title for *Shunnō-den: Tenchō hōju-raku* (Fascicle 2, p. 47) According to ZKKS, only the *Quick* of *Katen* was Chinese music, to be called '*Katen*', and transmitted by Sadatoshi. ZKKS also firmly states that the Hayashi who invented the dance was not a Chinese, and that his name is properly Naokura 直倉 *not* 眞倉 . The text adds the further detail that *Katen* was performed in China on the birthday of the emperor.

An occasion when *Katen* was performed in Japan – and again in the reign of Horikawa-in (Fascicle 1, p. 56) – as part of the celebrations when the emperor was visiting his predecessor, the ex-emperor, is described in the *Kokon-chomonjū* (Eckardt 1956, p. 89). The best dancer of his generation, Koma no Mitsusue 狛光季 (1025-1112) proposed *Katen* in place of '10,000 years' *Manzairaku* 萬樂 , on the grounds (a) that the emperor sees '10,000 years' every year; (b) that *Katen* is quite as suitable for a celebration; (c) that *Katen* is much more interesting as a dance; and (d) that the *palace* (the *Kanin* 閑院) was new (it had just been rebuilt).

Prefaces to the piece from the sources in tablature

KF/HSFRK

'The Palace of Congratulations' : New music. There is a dance. the dancers emerge with the *Way-Walking Michiyuki*, when retiring blow the *Quick* of the said piece. 賀殿・新樂・有舞・以道行出入時吹當曲急

SSSTF

'The Palace of Congratulations': ten measures; four times. 賀殿　拍子十　　四反

2 I am indebted to Professor Li Chunyi 李純一 of the Central Institute for Music-Research, Beijing, for this reference
3 YFSJ, pp. 1184, 1185 (reference from Professor Li Chunyi).
4 Reference from Professor Li Chunyi.

21

JCYR, SGYR

'The Palace of Congratulations' 賀 (some make it 嘉). *Broaching*: ten drum-beats [measures]; should be plucked = played four times. 'The score for transverse-flute' of the Lord Cho shu = Hakuga fue-fu states: 'But do not add strokes.' 賀或作嘉　破拍子十　可彈四反　長秋卿横笛譜云但不加撤

Quick: 20 drum-beats; should be played four times; in the last repeat add drum-beats. 'The score for transverse-flute' of [Prince] *Nangū*[5] says: 'Strike three-times beats.' 急拍子廿可彈四反終帖加拍子　南宮横笛譜云打三度拍子

Altogether 120 [= 4×10+4×20] drum-beats [= measures]. Nowadays the *Broaching* is played twice; at the end of the final repeat advance the drum in the [last] two measures. 合拍子百廿今世破彈二反　終帖末二拍子上太鼓

In the fourth repeat of the *Quick*-dance [there is] *Sara-i-zuki;*[6] in the same Section [= repeat] add drum-beats. 急第四反[7]舞更居突同帖加[8]拍子
井ヅキ サラ

When abbreviating, play the *Broaching* once and advance the drum in the last two measures. As to the *Quick*, play three times from then onwards; but when playing second and third repeats, in the final Section add beats. If playing only once, from the eleventh measure [onwards] advance the drum. 略時破彈一反　末二拍子上大鼓　急彈三反以下但[9]彈二三反時終帖加拍子　彈一反時從第十一拍子上大鼓

5 The citations in quick succession, taken from *Chōshūkyō ōteki-fu* and *Nangū ōteki-fu,* show plainly that in Moronaga's day both Prince Sadayasu's score and that of Minamoto no Hiromasa (Hakuga) were available for consultation, and that their annotations to *Tōgaku* pieces (little trace of which survives in the *Hakuga fue-fu* copies available today) were not necessarily identical.

6 A statement concerning *Sara-i-tsuki (sic)* also occurs at the end of RMS's account of *Katen,* associated with the retiring of the dancers. RMS adds that this is a matter requiring to be made certain. See later.

7 SGYR 遍　　8 SGYR inserts 加　　9 SGYR inserts 但

When the dancers emerge, play the *Quick* of 'The Bird'; when they retire, play again the *Quick* of the said piece. 舞出時彈鳥急入時重彈當曲急

When the dancers face South, add drum-beats. The retiring musics of other pieces are all effective with this. 舞人南向時加拍子＃他曲入樂皆効此

Middle-sized piece. New music.
中曲　　　　　新樂

The *Score for transverse-flute* of Prince Southern-Palace states: 'This piece derives from the time when Magistrate Fujiwara no Sadatoshi, sent to Tang [-China] in the Jōwa [reign-period], played [it] on the lute. When by imperial decree the dance was created, the *Broaching* was made from *Kashōraku;* the *Quick* was made from *Katen* 嘉殿; the "emerging-flute"[10] was made from the *Quick* of *Karubin* [= *Karyōbin* = *Tori*]. 南宮横笛譜云此曲承和遣唐時判官藤原貞敏彈テ琵琶來有動作　舞時以嘉祥樂爲破以嘉殿爲急　以伽婁賓急爲出笛也

The reader will have noted an overlap between this preface and the texts both of RMS and of KKS (see p. 20). The last passage in the preface, cited from the *Nangū ōteki-fu,* beginning 'Kono kyoku...' and continuing for the space of 19 lexigraphs, and the following passage, describing the use of various pieces made by the choreographer, occur almost verbatim in KKS; and the preface and KKS give the Chinese characters for the mysterious *Sara-i-tsuki* of RMS. According to KKS, the phrase should be written 更居突 ; but the preface shows 竊 instead of 突 . Editors do not attempt to explain the term, but it has the appearance of abbreviated dance-notation – perhaps deriving from 更落居突 *sarani-ochiiru-tsuku,* a sequence of the standard dance-movements, 'sitting down' and 'thrusting with the foot', or *plié* and *stamp.*

10 This term has not been seen elsewhere. Its use supports the notion that a *Processional*-movement may on occasion have been played by flute alone (Fascicle 1, p. 19).

WAY-WALKING Michi-yuki/Dao-xing
KF/HSFRK

Way-walking: Eight measures. In *Slow four-beats* play the *Quick* of 'The Bird' 道行．拍子八．延四拍子吹鳥急

BROACHING   Ha/Po 破

1 JCYR (left)

2 SGYR (left) 'use it in the second repeat and subsequently.'

3 JCYR: sharpening-dot supplied.

4 SGYR (right) 'one version states.'

5 SGYR (right) 'Southern bamboo' *Nanchiku* [*-fu*] 南竹 [譜], the score compiled by Prince Sadayasu (Wolpert 1977, see p. 135, n. 58). His flute-score is commonly referred to as *Nangū-fu* 南宮譜 or *Nanchiku-fu* 南竹譜

23

6 SGYR (left) *Katsura-fu* 桂譜 – a score linked with one of the sons of Hakuga (Minamoto no Hiromasa; see Marett 1976).

7 SGYR (right) 'one version states'.

8 SGYR (left) *Nanchiku* [-*fu*].

9 SGYR (right) *Katsura-fu*.

10 JCYR: ligature supplied, making a simultaneous octave.

11 SGYR (left) *Nanchiku* [-*fu*].

Variant *Broaching* (同曲 *Dō-kyoku/ Tong-qu* 'same piece')

Kakko-beats (*kobyōshi*) and *hyaku* are shown in both zither and lute parts, above and below the stave, respectively.

Taiko-beats (large hollow circles) below the lute part in measures 9 and 10 are original and presumably mark the onset of 'three-times' beats from the bass drum. This marking may be regarded as in accordance with 'advancing the drum in the last two measures' (JCYR, SGYR, p. 22).

1 JCYR (left) 'use it in the second repeat and subsequently.'

2 SGYR (left) 'use it in the second repeat and subsequently.'

3 SGYR (left) 'one version states.'

4 JCYR: ligature supplied.

5 JCYR: sharpening-dot supplied.

QUICK Kyū/Ji 急

1 KF/HSFRK: The annotation *ro on* 口音 is not understood. *Ro* is the graph used in flute tablature for *d'* as opposed to *d"* (六). The two lexigraphs appear to mean 'the *d'*-note', but this note is not obtainable on the mouth-organ *(shō/sheng)*, the lowest note of which is *a'*.

27

2 SGYR (left)  'one version states'.   3 JCYR: ligature supplied.

Preliminary comments on the structure of the suite

Notwithstanding the fact that *Katen* is set out as two movements only (save in KF/ HSFRK), of which but one is said to have come from China, the piece was evidently treated as a suite in the ninth century, with borrowed *Processional, Broaching,* and *Quick* as its constituents.

Inspection of *Broaching* and *Quick* suggests, perhaps, that the latter (*Katen* itself) is more fluent, more natural, more convincing, as a tune than is the *Broaching;* but the *Quick* itself is anomalous in organization, as compared with other *Tōgaku*-pieces. A structure of 20 measures of $\frac{2}{2}$ is less usual than, say, one of 16 measures; and within this 20, the melody does not segment regularly into a 4×5, **ABCB** structure, such as was seen in measured movements of *Shunnō-den,* for example (see later, p. 00). The construction by phrases can be represented as **ABCB'** ; but in this instance only **A** and **B** are 5-measure groups, while **C** and **B'** are 4 and 6 measures in length, respectively. Within this structure, however, **A** and **B** share a 2-measure sub-unit; and **B'** shares four of **B**'s measures, as shown diagrammatically in Figure 2.

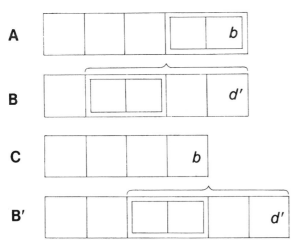

Figure 2

The regular alternation of *b* and *d'* as cadences of a minim-duration is a notable feature and is more characteristic of Chinese *gong-diao* modality (pentatonic: 1 2 3 5 6; with submediant, but lacking a sub-final) rather than *shang-diao* (pentatonic: 2 3 5 6 1, with flattened sub-final). Indeed, even in the heptatonic Mixolydian mode on D, *b* should be an auxiliary (a *bian*-note) and theoretically cannot function as cadence to a musical line.

The structure of the *Broaching*, in ten measures of $\frac{4}{2}$, is again irregular. Respecting cadences of a minim duration, the melody segments into phrases of 2, 4, 2, and 2, measures, with cadences on *a, d', a,* and *d',* respectively; but in this instance, and unlike the *Quick,* repetitions of material between phrases never extend to much more than half-measures. Representing successive *measures* (not *phrases*) by letters, the structure can then be summarized as follows (musical line-finals being shown in brackets):

A	B	*(a)*
A'	C	
D	E	*(d')*
F	B'	*(a)*
E'	E"	*(d')*

From the standpoint of melodic movement rather than structure, the *Quick* is also unusual in that the first two measures consist of notes from a broken triad: *f#' a' d".* Again, such a structure is more likely to occur in a Chinese pentatonic *gong*-mode; it is impossible in a pentatonic *shang*-mode. In a heptatonic *shang*-mode, the appearance of the mediant (in theory, an auxiliary), taken by leap, three times in the space of eight equal notes is surely anomalous.

Part of the attractiveness of *Katen* from the dancer's point of view, and as an alternative to *Manzairaku,* must have been not merely the music of *Broaching* and *Quick* but the fact that, while the *Modal Prelude* of *Ichikotsu-chō* was played as a preliminary, the procession to the dance-stage was executed (see RMS) to the *Quick* of 'The Bird' *Tori* 鳥 (an alternative name for 'Kalaviṅka': *Karyōbin/ Kalingpin* 迦陵頻;迦 is today pronounced *jia* in Chinese, but was used for the transcription of Sanskrit *ka*) (p. 30). This tune is one of the most delighful in the *Tōgaku* repertory. RMS states that the dance for the *Broaching* was lost — that is, by 1133; but KKS states that one 'time' of the *Broaching* is usually danced — that is, in the thirteenth century — while a second 'time' is a 'secret piece'.

6
Suite:
'The Bird'
Tori/Niao
鳥
or
'The *Kalaviṅka*'
Karyōbin/Kalingpin
迦陵頻[1]

Foreword to the piece

'The Bird', is surely one of the most attractive items in the *Tōgaku* repertory, both in respect of the melody of the *Quick,* and in respect of the dance by wing-bearing virgin boys, clapping shallow cymbals. The piece is also of particular interest in being linked with other pieces in ceremonies of which detailed accounts as early as the ninth century have survived. Again, like the *Bird Tune* of 'The Singing of Spring Warblers' (Fascicle 2, p. 67), the *Quick* of 'The Bird' is in some measure a contrafactum of birdsong and, more specifically, the song of a bird that delivers cuckoo-like calls as elements of its song.

The title and its significance

'The Bird' is a convenient shorthand and comprehensible Japanese reference, equivalent to the Chinese transliteration of the Sanskrit *Kalaviṅka* – a *bird* of a very special kind, both real and mythical. A variety of transliterations using Chinese lexigraphs are recorded. The most lengthy form, closest to *Kalaviṅka,* seems to have been written 迦陵頻伽 *Ka-liəng-b'iĕn-ka*[2], defined as 'a bird of melodious voice, found in the valleys of the Himalayas', possibly a cuckoo; but the name is also related to that of 迦頻闍羅王 Kapin-jalarāja, a previous incarnation of Śakyamuni as a pheasant. Schafer (1963, pp. 103, 104) firmly identifies the bird as

Dicrurus (or *Dissemurus*) *paradiseus,* the Paradise Drongo, with deep blue, metallic plumage, and a high resonant voice, perhaps the best bird-singer in the East. It occurs both in India and in the Indian Archipelago.

History of pieces of this, or related, title

The title is not known to the Chinese sources, and its first appearance in a Japanese document is probably that in the collection of records relating to the history of the Tōdaiji, the great temple at Nara, the collection known as *Tōdaiji-yōroku* 東大寺要錄[3]. At the reconsecration of the vast bronze image, during a second 'eye-opening' ceremony (the head having fallen off in 855) in 861:

While a eulogy is being recited, the elephant of Fuken/Puxian Bodhisattva (Samantabhadra) dances on the magnificent terrace. When the dance ends, the Horse-King [perhaps the horse-headed Kuan-yin,[4] *Hayagriva,* 馬（頭明）王, repelling evil spirits] takes up position, facing North. *Kalubinka* [= *Kalaviṅka*] in two facing rows [then] take up position and perform. (Note in the text: The one who newly made the dance is a Tang [-Chinese] dance-master, a certain 'Fuyafu' (in residence); the one who newly made the tune is a flute-master, a certain Wanibe no Ōtamaro.[5]

誦讚之間普賢并象王臺上舞畢馬王北面而立伽陵頻伽二
行對立奏（新造舞唐舞師某位父屋富（宿子）新造音聲笛師
某位和邇部大田麿）

1 For graphic variants see the discussion of the title, p. 30.
2 These are the so-called 'Ancient' or 'Middle' Chinese sounds as restored by Karlgren (1957); see 15a, 898c, 330a, 15a. The script-forms are those in Soothill and Hodous (1937); see p. 317a.
3 Printed in *Zoku-zoku-gunsho-ruijū* 續續羣書類從 (1907); see *maki dai-3* 卷第三, p. 54, columns 18-20.
4 See Soothill and Hodous (1937), p. 34la.
5 See Fascicle 1, p. 19.

From the manner in which this text is set out, it is plainly (as stated by Demiéville 1925, see p. 202) an hour-by-hour, diary account of the ceremony. Although the *dance* is a new creation attributed to a resident Chinese, and the *tune*, a new tune, or a revision, by the famous flute-teacher and performer of the reign of the Emperor Nimmyō, there is, already at this date, an association with the state of Rin'yū/ Linyi 林邑 Champa, attested by a later passage in the same text:[6]

First in order, the Rin'yū and foreign[7] musics [entered] from the central doorway on the South side; when, combined, they had sounded together, they thereupon entered each beneath his tent. (Note in the text: Rin'yū, namely, into the second tent to the East; foreign music, namely, into the second tent to the West.) At noon [at the end of the second thirty-minute period (*koku* 剋) of the two-hour interval beginning at 11 a.m. (午)] Rin'yū-musicians, birds,[8] and others from our monastery, holding up, respectfully, in both hands, offerings, etc., separately passed across the dance-terrace and entered into the hall. At the same time there was a man with a white elephant who took up position before [the hall]. This elephant, by means of the steps [reading 階 for 皆], reached [reading 搆 for 構] the dance-terrace.[9] A Bodhisattva was put on it. The white elephant was detained on the dance-terrace to await the time when those making offerings to the Buddha returned from the hall and, having participated in the dance, withdrew then to their own seats.

上次林邑胡樂自南中門參入共聲了進各就幄下（林邑就東二幄 胡樂就西二幄）午二剋本寺林邑樂人鳥等捧供盛物等東西分經 傶臺參於堂上奉即有一人白象立於前其象皆搆傶臺到菩薩於 其上白象拘留於傶臺待佛供者自堂還共傶了退下就本座

The presence of a type of *bugaku* – dance-with-music – entitled 'Champa-music' *Rin'yū-gaku,* is attested already for the year 752, in the account of the first eye-opening ceremony, in the same *Tōdaiji-yōroku,* by a mention of 'three dances of Champa-music' 林邑樂三舞 (*maki dai-2,* p. 42).

Champa, a state comprising the territory of Central and Southern Vietnam, first appears in Chinese sources in the third century AD as the kingdom of Linyi, founded about AD 192. The first inscriptions in Sanskrit appear in the third quarter of the fourth century (Coedès 1948, e.g. pp. 77 ff.). By the Japanese, Rin'yū/Linyi/Champa was regarded as an Indian kingdom, and the 'dances of Champa-music' as of Indian origin.

A comprehensive statement of this, the traditional view of the status of *Rin'yū-gaku* was given, for example, by Takakusu Junjirō 高楠順次郎 (1907) in an account of

the voyage of Kanshin/ Jianzhen 鑑眞 , a Chinese Buddhist of great distinction, from China to Japan, (Takakusu 1929, pp. 26-9). Kanshin arrived at Nara in 754, and there are no grounds for doubting the presence in his entourage of a Malay sculptor, a man from Champa, and priests from Sogdiana (胡國). Kanshin himself died in 763, and it was a pupil, Aomi no Mabito Genkai 青海眞人元開 , who composed an account of the voyage in 779. This account survives and is translated by Takakusu.[10]

An even earlier contact with Champa is attested, according to Takakusu, by the account of a Japanese mission, led by Tajihi no Mabito Hironari 多治比 眞人廣成 , which left Japan in 732 and returned in 735. On its return the members of the party are said to have included a certain Bodai-Senna (Bodhisena), a Brahmin from Southern India, and a musician from Champa, Buttetsu. Demiéville noted, however, that while the presence of Bodai is confirmed by two passages in the *Shoku Nihongi* 續日本紀 (the official history), that of Buttetsu is not. However, Lord Long-Autumn's *Score for transverse-flute* (a reference from the *Jinchi-yōroku* preface to *Karyōbin* – see p. 33 – not understood by Demiéville, who was able to see only extracts in the *Gakubube* 樂舞部 volumes of the *Koji ruien* 古事類苑 , 1931-6) mentions Buttetsu in association with Bodai, and this source cannot be later than 966, the date when Minamoto no Hakuga completed the compilation of his *Shinsen gaku-fu* – the proper title for Lord Long-Autumn's *Score.* It is untrue, therefore, that the name of Buttetsu is unattested before the twelfth century, as Demiéville states. Nevertheless, his main criticism of too trusting an acceptance of the view that any of this music is literally music from a kingdom in South-East Asia remains valid.

Demiéville had first been alerted to the weaknesses in this view by a critical article by Tsuda Sōkichi (1916)[11] and acknowledged his indebtedness in his own study, published in 1925. As we have seen, in the case of *Karyōbin* at least, the dance, at its first recorded performance in the ninth century, is said to have been 'made' by a Chinese, while the music is said to have been 'made' by a Japanese. Although associated with Champa-music then, it cannot itself be described as 'dance-music of Champa', save in some highly qualified sense, as yet undefined.

The testimony of the tenth-century *Wamyō-ruijū-shō* (Fascicle 1, p. 35) to the existence of Buttetsu has also to be rejected on the grounds that the entire section entitled *Kyokuchō-rui* 曲調類 , with its notes on pieces in the *Tōgaku*-repertory, appears to have been added at a date subsequent to the compilation of the first recension in five scrolls (*maki*)

6 *Zoku-zoku-gunsho-ruijū,* p. 59, columns 15-19.

7 Demiéville preferred to read *ko* 胡 'foreign' as *ko* 古 'old'; see Demiéville (1925), p. 203, n. 1. A discussion of this matter lies outside the scope of the present enquiry; it is, however, certain that the Japanese were familiar with the use of *ko* 胡 in reference to the inhabitants of Sogdiana, during the Nara period.

8 A first reference to the bird-dancers of *Kalaviṅka.*

9 Demiéville, accepting the printed text as it stands, confessed himself uncertain of the meaning. The emendations are those of L.E.R.P.

10 *Account of the Great Buddhist Priest's Eastern journey (Tang Daheshang dongzhengzhuan* 唐大和尚東征傳 , in *Gunsho-ruijū, maki dai-69,* pp. 540-56. See Takakusu 1930, pp. 47ff. for the account of the departure for Japan and arrival in Nara.

11 Tsuda, Sokichi 津田左右吉 , *Concerning Champa-music* 林邑樂に就いて , in *Toyogaku ho* 東洋緊報 , 6(1916), pp. 257-72.

for which the order for compilation was given between 923 and 930 (Demiéville, 1925, p. 209, n. 1, col. 2).

In explanation of the development of an association of a number of pieces with Champa-music, Demiéville suggested that the prestige of the *Daianji*-temple at Nara, with which the *Rin'yū*-music seems first to have been associated, progressively attracted to that tradition pieces that were mostly neither Chinese nor Korean in origin (though in one instance, in the case of *Ranryō-o,* a piece that was certainly Chinese): 'Pour un bouddhiste, indianiser est oeuvre pie; et le Rinyū était en Inde'. (Demiéville, 1925, p. 214). *Batō, Bairo, Karyōbin,* and *Bosatsu,* were all (according to the *Taigenshō,* 1510-12, Fascicle 1, p. 35) Rin'yū-music transmitted by Buttetsu; but Demiéville suggests rather that they were brought to Japan by one or other of the many musicians or priests who travelled from China to Japan during the Nara period; that they came neither from South-East Asian Champa nor from India, neither by the hand of Bodai nor by that of Buttetsu; that all were tenuously linked together by the use of the so-called Rin'yū *Free-tune (Ranjō)* when the dancers emerged and retired. (Regarding the Rin'yū *Free-tune* see n. 12 below and p. 47.)

The association of *Karyōbin, Jūtenraku,* and *Kochō/ Hudie* 蝴蝶 , with flower offerings, reminds Demiéville (p. 220) of dancers of the Chinese *Jiaofang,* reported in the *Songshi* 宋史 , the *Song History:* 'a file of Bodhisattvas offering flowers', a feature (as we have seen) of occasions when *Bosatsu* and *Karyōbin* were performed as components of one splendid ceremony. If indeed the piece *Karyōbin,* created in Japan, was classified as Rin'yū-music that heading must have denoted – as Demiéville urges – a genre or style, rather than the region of origin. He goes on to suggest that the development in China of the practice of accompanying *dances* from the state of Funan (contiguous to Champa) by Indian instruments (rather than Funan instruments – Funan was today's Campuchea), during the Tang, led to a confusion with *Indian* dance-music. The fact that the original Funanese dancers and musicians, performing at court during the Sui Dynasty, had been captured at Linyi, may have added to the confusion and completed the equation: Linyi/Rin'yū = India. That the music, musicians, and dancers , of Funan appealed to Chinese taste is well attested.

It is argued then that, during the eighth century, a type of dance and music, called *Rin'yū-gaku/Linyi-yue* was introduced to Japan, and came perhaps from Founan *via* China. To this type were subsequently attached other pieces, such as *Batō,* and *Bairo,* the origin of which was obscure.

What emerges with certainty, however, is the fact that a *Karyōbin* piece, *Kalubinka,* was played and danced at the second eye-opening ceremony at the *Tōdaiji* at Nara in 861; that the dance was devised by a Tang-Chinese, while the 'tune' was 'made' by the famous flautist Wanibe no Ōtamaro (798-865). Stylistically, the piece is as 'Chinese' as are other items in the *Tōgaku*-repertory.

Although the section on Modal Classes of Pieces in the *Wamyō-ruijū-shō* may not be regarded as of the tenth century (see Demiéville 1925, p. 209, n. 1), the entry relating to *Kalaviṅka* (*Karōhin* 迦樓頻) includes information not given elsewhere:

Some scores state: Indian language [Sanskrit]. The Chinese say that at the time when the Bird of Teaching sings, in its song it transmits the meaning of the emptiness of suffering: in the absence of that which commonly gives me pleasure, I am purified. Therefore its name: 'Bird of Teaching'. It is the Bird of the Pure Land of Highest Pleasure. Sarasvatī's pure country of Southern India transmitted this dance. [The High Priest] Sōjō Baramon seeing it, transmitted it. Later it was not retained in the territory of Tang. It first came to this country and was handed down.

Even if this section is as much as a century later in date than the date of compilation of the work in its original state, it still associates 'The Bird' with the Brahmin Buddhist High Priest. Whether this is an earlier testimony of association than that of *Ryūmeishō* cannot be determined until the date of first appearance of this information in *Wamyō-ruijū-shō* is known. It is of interest that this same text allocates the suite to the mode-key class *Sada-chō* 沙陀調.

Prefaces to the piece from the sources in tablature
KF/HSFRK

'The *Kalaviṅka*': old music. The dancers emerge to the *Free-tune* from Champa; they retire to the *Quick.* 賀陵賓 · 古樂 · 舞以林邑乱聲出以急入之
There is a dance. 有舞

SSSTF

'The Bird' *(Prelude)* 鳥序

Prelude: one Section of eight measures. 序一帖拍子八

Broaching: four times; eight measures. In the above mentioned *Broaching,* twice makes one Section.
破四反拍子八　件破以二反爲一帖
Old music.
古樂

Quick: eight measures. Last time, add drum-beats.
急拍子八　終帖加拍子

JCYR, SGYR

One name is *Karubin.* Some make *Karu-* into *Karyō-*; some make 賓 *(hin = bin)* into 頻 *(hin = bin)*
一名伽婁賓伽婁或作迦陵賓或作頻

Prelude: eight drum-beats [= measures]; should be played once. 序拍子八可彈一反

Broaching: eight measures; should be played six times; the last time, add drum-beats. The *Score for transverse-flute* of Prince Southern-Palace says: 'Should be blown four times.' Nowadays play twice. In the last time, from the third measure onwards, advance the bass-drum. 破拍子八可彈六反終帖加拍子|南宮横笛譜云可吹四反今世彈二 反終帖第三拍子以下上大鼓

Quick: eight measures. ⊥ne number of times is not fixed, but play following the dancers. When the dancers have made a great rotating circle and have returned to their original single file, strike 'three-times' beats. 急拍子八度數無定隨舞彈舞作大輪巡了復本列之時打三度拍子

When the dancers emerge, blow the *Free-tune* [= *Ranjō*] from *Rin'yū/ Linyi* 林邑 [= Champa][12] When retiring, play again (*kasanete* カサ子テ) the *Quick* of the said piece. 舞出時以林邑乱聲入時重彈當 曲急

Middle-sized piece. Music of Champa First blow the *Modal Prelude*. 中曲　林邑樂　先吹調子

While playing *Jūten-raku/ Shi Tian-yue* 十天樂 [13] 'Music of the Ten Devas', bird-dancers (six boys), hold vases of flowers, together with ten Bodhisattvas, holding flower-offerings, fire-vomiting serpents,[14] etc. Each of these two groups in two files passed across the dance-terrace and made offering to the Buddha. 奏十天樂之間鳥舞[15]童六人取花瓶並菩薩十人取花供火虵乚＝蛇丁等各兩行經舞臺之上供佛

Before the time of their retiring, the bird-boys first withdraw to the straw-lodge on the dance-terrace. Next, while the *Way-walking* is played, the files of Bodhisattvas return to station. When the dance is completed, they return and withdraw. Next, the birds take up station and dance. 前還時先鳥童退着舞臺上之草塾次吹道行之間菩薩行還立舞畢 還入　次鳥立舞

Nowadays, when the flower-offering is completed, at the time of return and withdrawal, Bodhisattvas and butterflies pass straight across the dance-terrace to the Music Room, the birds meanwhile staying in the straw–lodge on the dance-terrace. When the Bodhisattvas emerge, the birds come out from the straw-lodge and withdraw. 今世供花了退還時菩薩蝶直經舞臺入于樂屋鳥留着舞臺上之草塾　菩薩出時鳥起草塾退入

When the Bodhisattvas have danced, and after they have returned and withdrawn, the birds again emerge and dance. 菩薩舞了還入之後鳥更出舞

When the birds return and withdraw, the butterflies emerge and dance. 鳥還入蝶出舞

Lord Long-Autumn's *Score for transverse-flute* states: The piece is that which was originally transmitted by the Director of the Buddhist Ecclesia, the Brahmin Priest Bodai (Bodhi), together with Assistant-master Buttetsu, etc., etc. The said piece is danced together with the piece *Bosatsu/ Pusa* [= Bodhisattva]. Myōsen's *Score for transverse-flute*[16] states: 'The Bird' is the Bird of Paradise [= *Gokuraku-jōdo*]. In its song it sings the meaning of misery and unreality, of impermanence, etc. 長秋卿横笛譜云是僧正婆羅門僧菩提佛哲師木 [＝本？] 所傳云：件曲於菩薩共舞　明暹横笛譜云是鳥極樂淨土鳥也音中唱苦空無常等之義

It is [The Wonderful Sound of] *Myō-on-ten* [= female energy of Brahma] who subdued Southern India. 是妙音天降南天竺

The transmitter of this dance, the Brahmin Priest *(Baramon Sōjō)*,[17] observing that the tradition was not well established in the land of Tang, transmitted it directly to Japan. 傳此舞婆羅門僧正見傳不留唐地直傳日本也

12　The *Rin'yū-ranjō* has not survived in performance (p. 47); but Shiba 1972, vol. 4, pp. 178-201, 280, 281) transcribes a number of *ranjō* in *Ichikotsu-chō* and *Koma-ichikotsu-chō*, with the titles 'New music'-*ranjō* and 'Old music'- *ranjō*. The former tend to begin at the lower end of the octave range, the later at the upper end. What appears to be 'free' ('disordered' in the Chinese idiom *luansheng* 亂聲) about these flute-pieces seems to be their manner of performance, by three flutes, as canons in unison at a distance of one bar (as transcribed by Shiba).

13　This title does not occur, so far as is known, in any Buddhist context. The dictionary of Soothill and Hodous notes 'the twelve devas' 十二天 (of the Japanese *Shingon* sect) and also 'the twenty devas' 二十天 , and 'the twenty-eight heavens' 二十八天 . Moronaga's text makes plain, however, that the meaning of the title is 'Ten devas', since the music is associated in performance 'with ten Bodhisattvas holding flower-offerings'.

14　Misled by the lexigraphs 大虵 , in the *Koji-ruien* printed version of Moronaga's preface to *Tori* in JCYR *(Koji-ruien* 古事類苑 , 1931, *Gakubube* 樂舞部 , *Togaku gakukyoku jo* 唐樂樂曲上 , p. 389, column 5), Demiéville (1925) omits an apparent error; but both JCYR and SGYR have clearly 火虵 ; that is 火蛇 in standard forms. These (according to Soothill and Hodous) were 'fire-vomiting serpents in the hells' (1937, p. 162 a).

15　SGYR has, correctly, 儛 .

16　The date of this work is not known, nor does it survive. Myōsen is known as one of five great flautists of the early Heian period.

17　The *Baramon Sōjō/ Polomen Seng-Zheng;* see Demiéville, 1925, p. 209.

PRELUDE Jo/Xu 序

In order to display clearly the sequence of cadential notes at the ends of drum-beat periods, the score is shown with each such period on a single system. This does not of course imply any discontinuity between periods in performance.

---

1 Two sharps are bracketed in this signature because we do not know whether the flute made use of a Mixolydian note-set (with flattened seventh) or a Lydian note-set (with sharpened fourth).

2 JCYR (left): 'one version states

Asterisk marks where a ligature has been supplied, yielding a simultaneous octave.

3 SGYR (left): ' one version states.'

34

4 JCYR: sharpening dot supplied yielding a slurred ligature.   6 SGYR (left): '　　　 one version states.'

5 JCYR (left): 'one version states 　　　',

7 JCYR: ligature supplied yielding simultaneous octave.

8 JCYR: ligature supplied.

9 JCYR (left): 'one version states ,

Asterisk marks sharpening dot supplied, yielding a slurred

ligature.

10 JCYR (left): 'one version states ♪♪♪ Asterisks where simultaneous octaves result from slurs supplied.

11 SGYR (right): '♪♪ one version states.'

12 JCYR (left): 'one version states ♪♪♪'

13 SGYR (left): '♪♪ one version states.'

14 JCYR (left): 'one version states ♪♪'

The *Prelude* to 'The Bird' (as is evident from the preceding quasi-full-score) illustrates particularly clearly the greater reliability of the mouth-organ parts in general, as compared with the string parts, and the tendency for contraction of the string parts to occur owing to the apparent failure of scribes to copy repetition-signs.

No attempt has been made here to range consistently so that identical notes are invariably in vertical register on all staves within each system. It is clear that the length of certain drum-beat periods is greatest in the mouth-organ versions. One factor leading to shortening of periods in the string parts is failure to repeat the final note as a final binary unit; this happens in three of the eight drum-beat periods (**1, 3, 6**). Even when drum-beat cadences are shared by all parts, internal shortening of string-phrases seems to have been brought about by the omission of repetition signs. Periods **2** and **3** may have been shortened in the string parts in this way.

Of particular interest is the presence, in JCYR, of extended glosses in archaic flute-notation, so numerous as almost to furnish a complete version for flute. The style of tablature used is extremely archaic, with binary units delimited by the use of both *hiku* and *ichi* as markers (see Glossary), separately or combined, with *hiku* also used where a note is to be lengthened to yield a binary unit, or (in a single instance) dotted (see period **3**). The system of notation does not correspond to any one of the six Systems distinguished by Marett (1976, p. 38, Table III); but in

the use of *hiku* as binary marker the system resembles that of *Ko sō-fu* (Fascicle 2, p. 00). A single instance of the use of the quasi-glissando-sign *ren/lian* 連, ending in a mordent on the beat, it again a link with early flute tabulatures. As noted by Marett, this ornament is listed in HFF, though it does not occur in use in the body of the manuscript.

The observed condition of the parts for the various instruments, in the *Prelude* of 'The Bird', adds to the weight of accumulated observations on the *senza-misura, tempo-giusto Preludes* in the 'large pieces' (*daikyoku/daqu* 大曲) *Ō-dai hajin-raku* (Fascicle 1, pp. 43-64), *Toraden* (Fascicle 2, pp. 7–44), and *Shunnō-den* (Fascicle 2, pp. 45–71), that the music of such pieces, composed of drum-beat periods of varying numbers of binary units, was particularly susceptible to corruption, lacking (as it did) a fixed, repeating, metrical cycle, expressed in the percussion. Indeed, not a single *senza-misura, tempo-giusto Prelude* remains in the repertory of performed pieces at the present time.

The facts suggest that, of all musical aspects of the borrowed repertory, one that was most difficult for Japanese musicians to assimilate was the concept, precisely, of that type of *Prelude*. Conversely, on this reasoning, the notations of such unmeasured *Preludes* as survive are some of the most precious testimony for the archaic character of the *Tōgaku* repertory as a whole, for these are faithfully preserved relics, albeit incompletely understood, of the Tang tradition.

BROACHING Ha/Po 破

1. An upper marginal gloss in SGYR, over columns 1 and 2 of the *Ha/Po*, reads: 'At the third time, use the *d*-string; at the fourth time, use the *A*-string and from then on like this.' 第三遍用乚絃第四遍用 一絃次如此 The preface (p. 32) states initially that the *Broaching* is to be played *six* times, goes on to state that *four* times are recommended by Prince Southern-Palace but that 'nowadays' the movement is played twice. The upper marginal gloss evidently refers to the case when at least four and possibly more times are to be played. As the score shows, the *Broaching* begins on *d*; so that, as far as the lute is concerned, there is no change for the first three times. At the fourth time, however, the movement begins on *A*. A gloss in JCYR (n. 2) shows the piece beginning on *a'*; but no indications are given of how many times this is to be used. As shown by n. 3, however, even SGYR is by no means unambiguous in its instructions. Conceivably, the intention was to secure alternation of the initials *d A d A,* in four successive statements of the piece. The sign 夙 (SSTF, bars 7, 8) is not understood. 夕 might be an abbreviation of 殘 , perhaps 'withhold' (a secret tradition).

2. JCYR (right) [notation] Use it at the second time.'
   第二遍用之

3. SGYR (left) [notation]

4. JCYR: ligature ignored.

5. JCYR: ligature supplied.

6. JCYR: dots supplied, yielding a mordent.

7. JCYR: sharpening dot supplied.

8. JCYR: lower dot supplied, yielding a mordent.

9. JCYR (right) 'one version states [notation] .'

   Flute gloss: [notation] 中 夕

10. SGYR (right) 'one version states [notation] .'

11. SGYR (left) 'one version states [notation] .'

12. JCYR (right) 'one version states [notation] .'

13 SGYR (left) 'one version states [image: music notation] 火 .'

14 JCYR (right) 'one version states [image: music notation] .'

15 SGYR (right) 'one version states [image: music notation] 火 .'

16 SGYR (right) 'one version states [image: music notation] 火 .'

17 SGYR (left) 'one version states [image: music notation] 火 .'

18 JCYR (right) 'one version states [image: music notation] 火 .'

19 SGYR (right) 'one version states [image: music notation] 火 .'

Variant *BROACHING* Dō-Ha/tong Po 同破
('same *Broaching*')

The variant *Broaching* is present in JCYR and SGYR only. A singular feature (see n. 1) is the replacement, in both manuscripts, of solid *kakko*-dots (*kobyōshi*) by hollow dots in the third and fourth measures. Such dots have commonly been used, in Chinese and Sino-Japanese texts, to draw attention to some special feature of the text at

that point. An upper marginal gloss in SGYR refers to versions associated with the Northern and Southern capitals, and right and left glosses, associated with hollow dots, specifically draw attention to the practices of the Southern and Northern capitals (see nn. 6 and 8 below). The presence of this upper marginal gloss would seem to indicate that the gloss itself cannot be earlier than 1331, when the division between Northern and Southern capitals was established; this division lasted until 1391.

1 As marked, both manuscripts show hollow dots, instead of solid dots, as *kakko*-beat markers.
2 An annotation written in *katakana* beside this hollow dot reads, perhaps *hi yo* ヒよ 'a mistake, surely!', and presumably indicates that the hollow dot so marked is written there in error.
3 JCYR: ligature supplied.
4 SGYR: An upper marginal gloss (already referred to) is placed above columns 4 and 5 of the variant *Broaching* at this point: 'According to the Imperial traditions of the old music there

are two versions. These are, namely, the pair of versions of the two capitals, North and South. 古樂大上　有二說是南北二京兩也
5 JCYR: ligature supplied.
6 SGYR (right) 'Southern capital' 南京　; (left) ○
7 SGYR (right)
8 SGYR (left) 'Northern capital' 北京 , ○
9 JCYR: ligature supplied.
10 JCYR: ligature supplied.

41

The frequent occurrence of finger-plucked mordents within the space of a quaver/eighth-note in this variant in the *gakubyōshi*-style suggests that already, by late Heian times, the pace must have been no more than *Adagio*. By way of illustration of the probable effect in performance, the last measure of the variant is shown here, written out in $\frac{8}{2}$:

11 SGYR (left)   12 JCYR (right)

QUICK *Kyū/Ji* 急

1 SGYR (left) '  one version states.'

2 JCYR: ligature supplied.

3 SGYR (left) 絲竹譜 *Bamboo-Score*

4 SGYR: There is an upper marginal gloss over columns 3 and 4 of the *Quick*: 'The *Imperial*, and the *Katsura*, scores, the pair of [illegible] and other scores, all include two versions.'

Variant *QUICK dō-Kyū/tong Ji* 同急

('same *Quick*')

A variant of the *Quick* is present in JCYR only. The copyist seems to have omitted the equivalent of a minim/half-note from the beginning of the second measure. Small notes in the transcription suggest what may have been omitted. The regularity with which octaves fall on odd-numbered beats of the measure supports the reading suggested, and this requires the following *a* and *f#* be shortened to quavers/eighth-notes by the insertion of 'fire' *ka/huo* 火 .

7

Suite:
'The Eddying Bowl'
Kaibairaku/Huibeiyue

廻盃 *or* 杯樂

Foreword to the piece

Of items from the *Tōgaku* repertory so far considered, this is the second that consists now of a single movement only; but in this instance – unlike that of 'A Jade Tree's Rear-Court Blossom' – the evidence for the piece's having once formed part of a suite is unequivocal. Like some other items classed in the *Ichikotsu-chō* mode-key group, it is hexatonic, the flattened seventh – the characteristic feature of the Chinese *Yuediao* from which the *Ichikotsu-chō* derives – being absent.

The several sources in tablature rank it very differently in their order of pieces, JCYR/SGYR and SSSTF placing it in seventh place; KF/HSFRK, in sixteenth place.

History of pieces of this, or related, title

Concerning the history of this piece, very little is recorded in the Japanese handbooks; no performance is reported in *Kokonchomonjū* (KKCMJ). The title does not occur in the Chinese sources: JFJ, JGL, YFZL. Much more is available from Chinese sources regarding a seemingly related title: *Keibairaku/Qingbei-yue* 傾杯樂 'Tilting [=Draining] the cup' (in the *Taishiki-chō* mode-key group); but there is no reason to suppose there is any connection between the two. The meanings of the two titles are quite different. *Keibairaku* refers to the complete draining of a wine-cup achieved by turning it upside-down – 'bottoms up' in the vernacular. *Kaibai* literally means 'the returning, circulating, or revolving, bowl or cup'. It may have been applied to a beaker, passed from hand to hand round a company of drinkers; but it

might also (and, as will be shown, more probably) have been applied to a wine-cup floating on a stream, in a garden-banquet, perhaps spinning round, caught in an eddy.

The title is listed (in the form 廻杯樂) in the *Ichikotsu-chō* mode-key group, without comment, in the *Wamyō ruijū-shō* (WMRJS) as we now have it; but this entry, along with those for other *Tōgaku* titles, must be (as we have already seen, p. 31), later than the text of the tenth-century original of this work.

Again, Professor Li Chunyi (p. 21, n. 2) has drawn attention to a suggestion, in the *Ritual Music Monograph* (禮樂志) of the *Dainihonshi* 大日本史 ,[1] that 盃 might be an erroneous substitution for 波 , and in that case the piece might be related to or identical with the *Huibo-yue* 回波樂 , mentioned in JFJ, or the *Huipoyue* 回婆樂 , listed in JGL The possibility of these words – 坏 or 盃 , 波 , 婆 – being phonetic substitutes for each other becomes apparent when their Tang pronunciations, as reconstructed by Karlgren, are considered, namely: *b'uậi* (Karlgren 1957, 999 s.) or *puậi* (999o.), *puâ* (25 1.), *b'uâ* (25q.). The references to a *Huibo-yue* or *Huipo-yue* in JFJ and JGL respectively are supported by an entry in the YFSJ and, by accounts, in the

---

1 *Dainihonshi* 大日本史 , by Tokugawa Mitsukuni 德川 光国 and others, begun in the seventeenth century and completed in 1909, Tōkyō (1928-9): see 志 5, *maki dai* 347, p. 219, entry: *Kaibairaku*.

2 YFSJ in *Zhongguo gudian wenxue jichu congshu, di san ce* 中國古典文學基礎叢書第 三册, *Zhonghua shuju* 中華書局 (Beijing, 1979); j. 80, p. 1134.

46

Benshishi 本事詩 (BSS)[3], of the composition of lyrics for this tune. The tune itself seems to have been associated with an original song-text in lines of six lexigraphs of which the first was perhaps 'The Qushui wafts along the floating goblet' 曲水引流泛觴 . (At least three geographically distinct streams were known by this name of 'Twisting waters', in Jiangsu, Zhejiang, and Sichuan Provinces; and on these, cups of wine for guests were floated in the familiar gentle pastime.) Between them, YFSJ and BSS furnish three different song-texts to be sung to the *Huibo-yue* tune: YFSJ, a lyric by the Tang poet Li Jingbo 李景伯 ; BSS, a lyric by a disgraced but pardoned official, Shen Quanqi 沈佺期 , and in addition a lyric by an actor (a *yuren* 優人).

According to the preface to Li Jingbo's lyric in YFSJ, the *Tang History* states that it was in the reign-period Jinglong 景龍 (707-10) of his restoration that Emperor Zhongzong 中宗 (who also reigned for one year only in 684), at a banquet for the officials in attendance, ordered the making of song-texts for *Huibo-yue*. The preface ends with the statement that the Deputy Censor, Li Jingbo, then sang this lyric and later also made a dance-piece. In addition, YFSJ affirms that the *Huibo-yue* was a piece in a *Shang* (Mixolydian) mode made in the time of Zhongzong; but in fact the texts (YFSJ and BSS) only describe use of a *tune: Huibo-yue*, as a vehicle for *song-texts* made in the time of that emperor. The account, at the end of the BSS, of the composition of lyrics to be sung to the *Huibo-yue* indicates plainly that the tune was already in existence.

All three lyrics quoted in YFSJ and BSS are quatrains in lines of six lexigraphs, all three begin with the words *Hui bo*, with *hui* written as 回 or 廻 . These two lexigraphs share the meaning 'to return', but the latter (also written 迴) has the additional meaning 'to revolve' and 'to bend round and return'. From Shen Quanqi's poem, the meaning of *hui* 廻／廻 is 'to return', for he compares his own return to office with the action of the returning wave. Only Li Jingbo's poem continues the association with wine-drinking – 'On eddying waves, till now, the wine-bowls [floated]'; but the linking of the original *tune*, the *Huibo-yue,* with the original drinking song: *Qushui yinliu fan shang,* seems to have led to a meaningful substitution in the tune-*title* of a word meaning 'wine-cup' for a similarly sounding word meaning 'wave'. 'The returning wave *(puâ)*' may thus have become 'The returning bowl *(b'uâi)*', or 'The returning cup *(puâi)*'. (Further discussion of the relationship between the tune *Kaibairaku* as we have it and the tune to which these Tang lyrics were sung will be found on p. 52.)

Brief entries relating to *Kaibairaku* are to be found in RMS and KKS, and the prefaces to the piece contain, in some instances, important additional material. RMS gives the pronunciation of the title with great care: *ka-i-ba-i-ra-ku* 火いばいらく and states that it is New Music

(Fascicle 1, p. 35) in eight measures, to be played four times. 'It is known that there was a *Prelude*. However, this has recently been discontinued. Not even on the border [lacuna] is it to be heard.' KKS states that the *Prelude* consisted of a single Section in four measures, while the *Broaching* consisted of four Sections each of eight measures. (Here 'Section' probably means a 'time'.) The preface to the piece in JCYR and SGYR (p. 48) repeats this statement and adds that in the Jōwa reign-period (834-47 – that is, the beginning of the reign of the Emperor Nimmyō), those in palace circles were fond of this piece; but, according to KKS, by the time of the author Koma no Chikazane, it was played as 'ascension-music' *(togaku* 登樂*)* for Buddhist 'precentors' ('chant-masters') *baishi* 唄師 ; Sanskrit *Bhāṣā)* (see Nihon Shisō Taikei edn 1973, *maki dai* 6, p. 114, 23). The JCYR, SGYR preface states, however, that, according to old tradition, cited in the *Transverse-Flute Score* of Myōsen, the piece is used in association with many musical items as a 'Great Way-Walking' (*Dai Michiyuki* 大道行). A maximum of information about the structure of the original suite comes from the concise preface to the piece in KF/HSFRK (p. 48). This makes plain that what survives is indeed the *Broaching,* to be played four times, and that *Prelude* (twice) and *Quick,* together with the dance, had already become extinct *(taeru* 絶*)* when that manuscript was compiled – *c.* 1200.

Of the very greatest interest is a further piece of information given in this same preface in KF/HSFRK, namely that, when the dance was performed, the dancers emerged to the *Rin'yū-ranjō.* already referred to in relation to 'The Bird' (p. 32). As previously indicated, Demiéville pointed out that this Rin'yū *Free-tune* was linked not only with the performance of items associated with 'dance-music of Champa' but also with that of a number of pieces of obscure provenance. The linking of *Kaibairaku* with the Rin'yū *Free-tune* may have come about *either* because of some Buddhistic association – witness thirteenth-century use in liturgical processions – *or* because it was of uncertain, possibly exotic, origin.

Summarizing, then, it is certain that the piece is the surviving *Broaching* of a three-movement ballet-suite, popular at court in the ninth century, of which both *Prelude* and *Quick* are lost; and furthermore that this piece was one of those associated with use of the Rin'yū *Free-tune* as *Processional*.

As already noted, the *Rin'yū-ranjō* does not survive in performance today (p. 33, n. 12.) However, this and other *ranjō* are discussed in KKS (Nihon Shisō Taikei edn 1973, *maki dai* 1, p. 27), and there, miraculously preserved, is a *Rin'yū-ranjō* in flute tablature. KKS states quite simply that Rin'yū is a name for India, and of itself this link surely suffices as explanation of the fact that any piece associated with Buddhist ceremonies attracts to itself use of the Rin'yū *Free-tune*. The text immediately goes on to state that the notes *(kotoba* 詞*)* of this *Free-tune* are the same as those of the 'Old-music' *(Kogaku* 古樂 *) Free-tune.* 'The Tsu-no-suke 津介 (Second in command of harbours), Katsu

---

3 Meng Qi 孟啓 : (late ninth century) in *Yunji youyi* 雲谿友議 *Gudian wenxue chubanshe* 古典文學出版社 (Shanghai, 1957); see p. 24.

no Michinaru 勝道成 (Outer Junior Fifth Rank, Lower Grade)[4] has stated that: when this *Free-tune* is used, one does not start playing from the *roku* 丨丨 [low *d*] hole [the lower end of the flute's octave in Heian times]; but while the first time begins like this, mid-times begin from the low-*d* hole.' The text continues: 'Its notes are:' (*Sore no kotoba un* 其詞云), and the *Free-tune*, in flute tablature, follows. Intracolumnary hollow dots are printed in KKS as large as *taiko*-beat dots, and there are neither *hyaku* nor *taiko*-dots − as indeed is the case in modern *Free-tune* scores.

The use of *kotoba* in the two instances quoted here affords convincing evidence of that which has previously been urged, namely, that 'word' (*kotoba* 詞) is frequently used for 'note' in musical texts.

Since the modern *Tōgaku*-flute, *ryūteki*, no longer uses the lower end of its fundamental range, comparison between the KKS Rin'yū-*ranjō* and *ranjō* transcribed and published by Shiba is not readily possible. Nevertheless, as his transcriptions show (Shiba 1972, *maki* 4, pp. 178-87), whereas the 'New-music' *Free-tune* (as well as the 'Small') begin their melodies (after brief incipits) on the lowest 丨丨 (*d'*) in the flute range, the two 'Old-music' *Free-tunes* begin on *a'* or *b'*. To this extent, therefore, the surviving 'Old-music' *Free-tunes* are in conformity with Katsu no Michinaru's specification.

Here is a first transcription of the *Rinyū-ranjō* as given in KKS. Although it is metrically very different from what is now performed as *Kogaku-ranjō*, its melody relies heavily on the same small group of adjacent notes as the latter, but for the use of the low *d'*, namely, *f'*, *g'*, *a'*, *b'*, *c"*. Since the *Rinyū-ranjō* was used with pieces in the *Ichikotsu-chō* mode-key group, the transcription shows the *f'* sharpened and the *c"* natural.

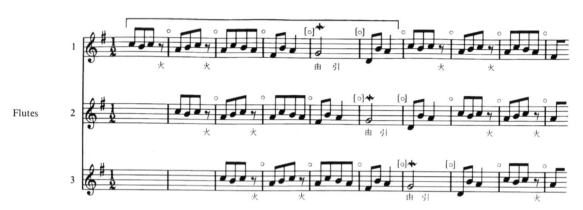

The bracket covers what the text gives in flute tablature; the addition of two more flutes in canon, in unison, at the distance of one binary unit is a suggestion made in the light of the modern manner of performance of *ranjō*. After the final intra-columnary hollow dot, the text adds: 'Play like this.'There follows the further statement: 'Not used today' − that is, in the thirteenth century.

Prefaces to the suite from the sources in tablature

KF/HSFRK

'The Eddying Bowl'
New music. *Prelude*, two Sections. Beats [= measures] of each

separate Section, eight. 新樂.序二条拍子条別八

When the dancers emerge: Rinyū *Free-tune* 舞出臨邑乱聲

There is a *Quick*. 有急

Nowadays the dance is extinct. *Prelude* and *Quick* are extinct. 今舞絶.序急絶

4 Katsu no Michinaru, a flute-player active in the first half of the ninth century, is mentioned by Hakuga in the postface to his *Shinsen gaku-fu* (see Marett, 1976 Figure 2 (facing p. 12), 67b, and pp. 12 and 19, n. 10). In view of the recorded use of the *Rin'yū ranjō* in 861 (p. 30), he was probably in a position to speak with authority regarding its musical characteristics.

Broaching, four Sections; measures in each, eight..破四条拍子別八

SSSTF

'The Eddying Bowl'
Eight measures. 拍子八

JCYR, SGYR

'The Eddying Bowl'
Prelude: one Section. Measures, four. No dance. The above-mentioned Prelude is completely extinct. 序 ·帖拍子四无舞件 序斷了

Broaching: Measures, eight. Sould be played four times. Together, measures amount to 32.[5] In the final Section [= time] strike three-times beats. 破拍子八 可彈四反 合拍子三十[5]二 終打三度拍子

A middle-sized piece. New music. 中曲 新樂

Southern-Palace's *transverse-flute score* states: In Jōwa times, palace circles were fond of this piece. 南宮横笛譜云承和御時殿上被好此曲

Quoting old tradition, Myōsen's *Score for transverse flute* states: Many musical items use it as a *Great Way-Walking*. 明暹横笛譜云古老傳云諸音樂大道行用之

5 SGYR correctly has 'thirty two'; JCYR has 'twenty two'.

BROACHING Ha/Po 破

1   JCYR: ligature supplied.

2   SGYR (left) ' one version states.'

3   JCYR: sharpening dot supplied yielding slurred ligature.

    (right) ' one version states.'

Variant *Broaching dō-Ha/tong Po*

Reconstruction of a tune for the surviving song-texts

As already observed, all three song-texts for *Kaibairaku/Huibo-yue* recorded in YFSJ and BSS are quatrains in lines of six lexigraphs, and in each case semantic rhythm would seem to require a metre of ♩ ♩ ♩ ♩ ♩ ♩ for the line – the same metre, indeed, as that of the lyric believed to have been the original lyric to which the *Huibo-yue* was sung. In Li Jingbo's lyric 'wine-goblet' *jiuzhi* 酒卮 [= 厄 ?] matches 'floating goblet' *fanshang* 泛觞 (both of large capacity!), at the end of the *Qushui*-line. For singing, one *note to one syllable, a musical line of two measures of four beats would suffice; but Kaibairaku,* as we have it, consists of four musical lines, each of two measures of eight. It appears then that, as in the case of *Gyokuju gotei-ka* (p. 17), the tune was already decoratively expanded (see the mouth-organ part) before it reached Japan.

In the light of the principles of melodic embellishment revealed by the flute version of *Ō-dai hajin-raku* (this fascicle, p. 53) a tune of eight measures of four has been restored. The principles recognized are the following: (1) within a binary unit of two notes descending by step, the second, unstressed note, is likely to be the original melody-note, since the commonest type of ornament is the appoggiatura; (2) within a binary unit of two notes moving by leap, the first, stressed, note is likely to be the original melody-note, since échappés are not stressed. Two ligatures in the first and third measures have been retained for the sake of melodic variety, and the penultimate lexigraph of each text-line also appears to have been sung to a ligature.

Although described in YFSJ as a Mixolydian (*Shang*) tune, no trace of a natural seventh appears in the mouth-organ part (or, of course, in the reduced melody). The Lydian lute part includes *c♯'*, but only as an appoggiatura to *b*, and there is no *c♮'* in the zither part. Evidently, however, only a minor change in the fourth and eighth measures would be necessary to give a Mixolydian flavour to the reduced melody. Such a change might be the substitution of a ligature: *d' c♮',* for the penultimate crotchet/quarter-note.

(1)	Qu -	shui	yin -	liu	fan	shang。					(YFSJ)
(2)	Hui	bo	er	shi	Quan -	qi。	Liu	xiang	ling	wai	sheng	gui。

(BSS, Shen Quanqi)

| (3) | Hui | bo | er | shi | kao - | lao。 | Pa | fu | ye | shi | da | hao。 |

(BSS, an actor)

| (4) | Hui | bo | er | shi | jiu - | zhi, | Wei | chen | zhi - | zai | zhen - | gui。 |

(YFSJ, Li Jingbo)

| 回 | 波 | 爾 | 時 | 酒 | 卮, | 微 | 臣 | 職 | 在 | 箴 | 規。 |

| Shi | yan | ji - | guo | san | jue. | Xuan - | hua | qie - | kong | fei | yi |
| 侍 | 宴 | 既 | 過 | 三 | 爵。 | 誼 | 譁 | 竊 | 恐 | 非 | 儀。 |

(YFSJ, Li Jingbo)

In the reduction of the *Kaibairaku*-melody shown here, four texts in transliteration are set as underlines to the notation: (1) the only recorded line from the original *Huibo-yue;* (2) two lines from the lyric by Shen Quanqi; (3) two lines from the lyric by an anonymous actor; (4) the lyric by Li Jingbo.[1] The Chinese text for the last is added below the transliteration. The text may be translated as follows:

On eddying waves till now the wine-bowls [floated].

This small officer, in his official capacity, now makes admonition:

While attending the banquet, already three pledging-bowls [have circulated]

[And this] bawling hubbub, I venture to think, lacks good manners.[2]

1 'Jingbo' is a courtesy name – a *zi* 字.

2 Dr Anne Birrell has again given help in the making of this translation.

'The Emperor destroys the Formations'

Flute-score of *Ō-dai hajin-raku* transcribed from *Kaichū-fu* (KCF)

The transcription that follows (p. 56) is set out in parallel with the single-stave, conflated version of the suite, based on a critical consideration of variants, as described in Fascicle 2, p. 72. Conflation and flute version are evidently in strikingly good agreement. From a musical standpoint, the transcription is important (a) because it shows how closely that instrumental voice in the *Tōgaku* ensemble which lay in highest tessitura followed the melodic line carried by the mouth-organ; (b) because it displays the several kinds of decorative procedure utilized in melodic embellishment by the flute. This is a first transcription, and, as with the flute part for *Gyokuju gotei-ka,* metrical revision may be necessary in the light of more recent studies.

A reading of the transcription reveals that the commonest decorative device is the insertion of appoggiaturas. Échappés, auxiliary notes, and, very rarely, anticipations also figure in the decoration of the melodic line, but these are used relatively infrequently. Mordents are more frequent than in the conflated version, and some of these are marked as double-shakes: 由二 . A new type of ornament, peculiar to the flutes, is the descending glide, indicated by the sign 連 . This frequently matches a mordent in the conflated version.

The measured *Broaching* shows that the *taiko-* and *kakko*-beats fall almost invariably on the *appoggiatura,* not on the original *melody-note.* Conversely, in the case of an échappé, the beat falls on the *melody-note* rather than on the *échappé.* Only rarely, as in the first two measures of Section 4 of the *Broaching,* is the *kakko*-dot marked beside the melody-note of the pair: appoggiatura + main note. These observations are important in that they show what was the accentuation of such grace-notes at the time when the tablature was devised and the manuscript written.

Turning now to the nature of the flute tablature in KCF, the score of *Ō-dai hajin-raku* shows that the principles according to which ornaments are notated are essentially the same as those adopted for the lute. The *Fushimi-no-miya hon biwa-fu* (Fascicle 1, pp. 10, 11, 12) refers already to ornamental notes by the striking metaphor of 'commentary notes' *chū-on/zhu-yin* 注音 .[1] In Sino-Japanese and Chinese texts, glosses were frequently written in smaller lexigraphs, and placed to the right of the main columns of the text. As shown by this usage in a passage from a lute-tutor and score, copied in Japan in 920-1, embellishments of a melodic line were thought of, by the Japanese, as musical glosses to a text. Accordingly, they were to be represented by smaller versions of the tablature-signs, written, as a commentary or gloss might be, to the right of the main column of the principal melody-notes. The resulting appearance of later Heian lute tablature can be seen in

Fascicle 1, Plate 4, (c), (d) (facing p. 31), where finger-plucked mordents, passing notes, and appoggiaturas are written smaller than, and to the right of, the main column of signs.

Inspection of two manuscripts of KCF, namely that from the Naikaku Bunko (see p. 00) and that from the Research Archives for Japanese Music of Ueno Gakuen College, Tokyo, shows that appoggiaturas to notes that are seen, from the conflated version, to be notes of the primary melody, are written as smaller-sized tablature signs, and that they are slightly displaced to the right, away from the column axis on which signs for primary notes lie. The conjunct groups, such as *b a g*, usually made conspicuous by the writing of *ren/lian* 連 'to connect; to join' following the last note, are commonly written with *b* and *a* in sequence, small, and to the right of the column axis, while *g*, of normal size, lies on the column axis. (See Plates 1 and 2.)

As in other manuscripts making use of other systems of tablature signs, the columns in KCF are segmented into binary units by intracolumnary hollow dots (Ueno Gakuen copy) or pairs of small solid dots in horizontal register (Naikaku Bunko copy). *Hiku* signs (引 reduced to リ) have various uses: they may be used to double note-durations and occasionally seem to have been retained as binary markers. They have yet another use, not previously met with in the notation of *Tōgaku* pieces, but noted by Dr Markham in Moronaga's string parts for the *Saibara* repertory; that is, they can be used as a dot, applied to the preceding tablature sign. (See the first drum-beat period of the *Prelude,* p. 57.) One rhythmic difference between the two versions (upper and lower staves) is to be noted, since it is repeated four times and must therefore be regarded as constituting an intentional variant. This occurs at the end of each of the first four Sections of the *Broaching.* The pitch-values of the notes are the same in both versions, but the rhythmization of the passage differs.

In general, the rhythmization of sets of notes within a binary unit is facilitated for the transcriber when differences in size between note and grace-note are evident, along with the placing of *kakko-* and *taiko*-beat dots. In movements without such dots, size differences alone are of even greater importance. Clearly, if copyists fail to maintain size differences, and fail to observe displacement of grace-notes from the column axis, rhythmic details can no longer be decided with certainly. Respect, on the part of the scribe, for distinctions between sizes of tablature signs, for placement of signs on the main column axis or to the right of that axis, and for the placing of *kakko-* and *taiko*-beat signs, are thus all three essential, if the tablature is to be read unambiguously.

In addition to any shortcomings in the conduct of

1 The passage is translated by Wolpert (1977), p. 150.

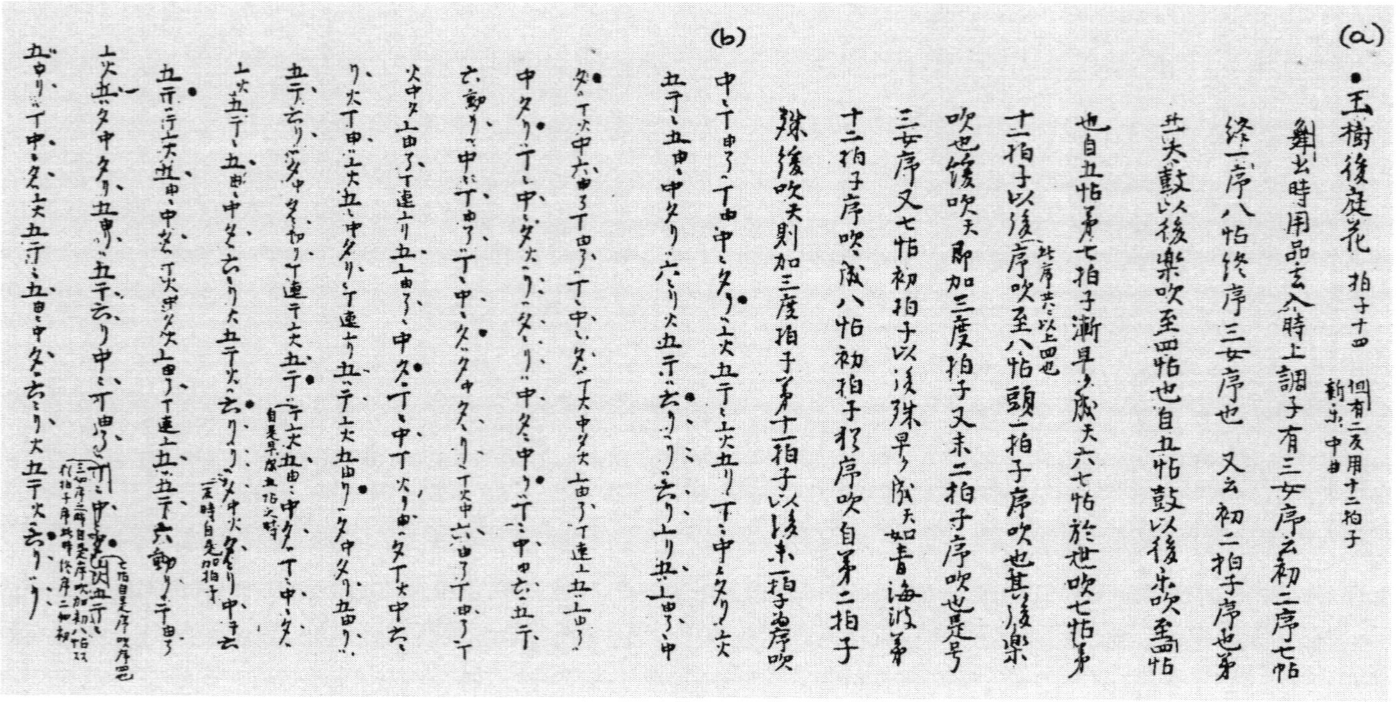

Plate 1 *Kaichu-fu* (1095?) (Naikaku Bunko 内閣文庫) (flute *ryūteki*) *Gyokuju gotei-ka*. From right to left (a) title and Preface, (b) notation of the piece, with glosses (see p. 15) relating to 'preludial' playing and 'three-times' beats.

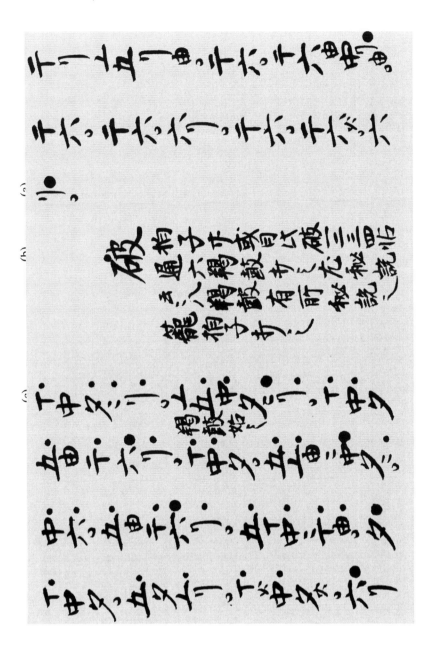

Plate 2   *Kaichū-fu* (1095?) (Ueno Gakuen, *Nihon ongaku shiryoshitsu*) (flute *ryūeki*) *Ō-dai hajin-raku*. From right to left (a) end of *Prelude*, (b) prefatory comments on the *Broaching*, (c) first six measures of the *Broaching*. Some say, as to Sections 1 to 4 of this *Broaching*, there is a secret version. Beat As to eight *kakko*-beats [to the measure], there is a secret version. Beat column of tablature-signs reads: '*Kakko* begins'. A Naikaku Bunko 1793 reads: 或目此 instead of 或曰此, to be translated, perhaps: 'Some, from this [point], beat six *kakko*-beats [to the measure] thoughout…'

Section (*fō*) of the *Broaching*. The Preface reads: '*Broaching*: 20 [bass-drum] beats. *kakko*-beats [to the measure] throughout; but a secret version states: it in *komebyōshi* [Fascicle 1, pp. 23, 65]'. The gloss to the left of the first copy of KCF (199 亞 163 號) copied in the year Kansei 5 (寬政五年), beat six *kakko*-beats [to the measure] throughout…'

55

copyists, for the musicians themselves, the distinction between main notes and grace-notes will have begun to be obliterated as the pace of performance was reduced, and the original tune ceased to be remembered. As can be heard in the performance of the Court musicians today, even the decorated melodies of flute and *hichiriki* are no longer grasped as melodic wholes by the performers; the decorated melodies have disintegrated into melodic fragments, in which micro-ornament, in the shape of pitch-glides, has become a primary focus of interest.

As shown by the transcription of 'A Jade Tree's Rear-Court Blossom' made by Dr Markham and Dr Wolpert (p. 12), some flute scores in KCF exhibit a more highly decorated melodic line than that of the flute version of *Ō-dai hajin-raku*. Dr Markham has observed that the KCF notations are closely similar to those of the *Chū Ō-ga ryūtekiyo-rōku-fu* (CORYF), and these in turn are closely similar to those of the flute parts, of Meiji date, printed and readily available today (see Fascicle 1, p. 6, n. 4). Inspection of Shiba's transcriptions – of *Katen no kyū/Hedian-ji* 賀殿急 , for example (Shiba 1972, *maki* 2, p. 101) – show that ornaments executed *on a kakko*-beat in KCF have come to be anticipated, so that their time-value is now subtracted from a *preceding* note. This observation notwithstanding, there can be no doubt that the flute-score of *Ō-dai* preserves the original condition of the decoration, with appoggiaturas *on* the beat and taking their value from the *following*, original melody-note.

With potential sources of imperfection in the flute manuscripts already recognized, it is clear that careful collation of source copies must be undertaken before the more elaborate flute parts can be read with confidence. Particular attention must be paid, in one and the same manuscript and one and the same piece, to variant treatment of the same passage of figuration on repetition, since there are grounds for accepting that such passages were originally notated in the same way. While accepting the need for detailed future collation, our transcriptions of *Ō-dai hajin-raku* and *Gyokuju gotei-ka* may stand as tentative, preliminary readings.

In an upper-marginal gloss, the practice of repeating the *Processional*, from the beginning, is marked as an oral tradition; but a further note adds that other versions 'have a play-again place' 有返吹所 – in Western terms a marked *Dal segno*. Unlike the earlier scores in tablature, transcribed in Fascicle 1, the KCF-manuscript marks '*kakko*-beginning' on the first *a'* of the *Processional*. Furthermore, in each of the Sections 1 to 5 of the *Broaching*, an annotation states that the *kakko* begins in the second binary unit of each Section. In Section 4, three *taiko*-beats are given their serial number within the Section, together with the number of *kakko*-beats associated with each *taiko*-beat: 13th/4 *kakko*: 14th/8 *kakko*; 15th/4 *kakko*. These annotations show plainly that the *taiko*-beat itself was also counted as a *kakko*-beat in the definition of what, in the West, would be regarded as a measure. (A colophon relating to various alternative lengths of performance of the *Prelude* has not been translated.)

PROCESSIONAL

PRELUDE

1 [The next] four drum-beat [periods] are frequently danced
 to. Therefore they should be played. 拍子四常舞之仍可吹之

59

Kohanjō

61

BROACHING
Section 1

Section 2

2 'From here onwards blow [= play] like a *Prelude* '已下序吹

Section 3[4]

3 'There is a variant: [notation] Where this variant is to be fitted in is not clear. It follows the end of Section 2 in two columns of tablature, prefaced by 有説

4 'Of drum-beats, 20. At the end play four preludial drum-beat

[periods]. There are two places with five *kakko*-beats.' 拍子廿末序吹四拍子五羯鼓有二所

5 'There is a variant: [notation] This variant is: that the first measure has seven [*kakko*-] beats.' 物拍子七拍子説是之(?)

64

Section 4[6]

6 'Of drum-beats, 20. At the end play four preludial drum-beat
[periods]. There are two places with four *kakko*-beats.
Frequently not used.' 拍子廿末四序吹四羯鼓二所常不用之

65

Section 5[7]

7   'Of drum-beats, 20. Play like a *Prelude*. According to an old variant, the fifth Section is said to be played in the "music-blowing" [manner]. Furthermore play [Sections 5 and 6] joined together." 拍子廿序吹之古說二八五帖樂吹云二尚連吹

Section 6[9]

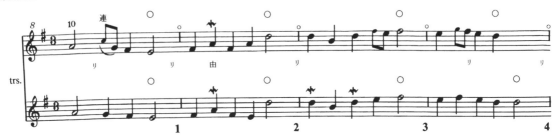

8 'A secret oral tradition states that when the flute graciously
plays, the sixth Section is to be played joined [to Section 5].
A variant to be kept secret. 秘口傳云笛下之天吹，時又六
帖吹連之可秘說

9 'Of drum-beats, 20. To be played like a *Prelude*. Play joined
[to Section 5]. Oral tradition states limits kept! 拍子廿序吹
之連吹之口傳聊程置歟

10 'The *Arei tanshō* [= short tune] begins [here].' 阿禮短聲始

67

11 The manuscript concludes with a note on possible abbreviations
of dance and performance.

On *Toraden* 'The Whirl-Around' and *Shunnō-den* 'The Singing of Spring Warblers'

Justified, single-stave conflations of two instrumental suites (N.J.N.)

The two dance-suites of Fascicle 2 have extended knowledge of music from the Tang Court and added to our appreciation of the quality of this ancient, imperial entertainment music. What was said in Fascicle 2 about the rationale and the methods of achieving a justified, single-stave conflation of *Ō-dai hajin-raku* 'The Emperor Destroys the Formations', stands firm in the present approach to *Toraden* and *Shunnō-den*: 'to allow the music to be seen and heard at length... for further study in purely musical terms', and 'to devise a conflated version in which all essentials of the various sources are retained, all differences weighed up in the light of circumstances, and a solution reached acceptable for a specifically musical purpose' (Fascicle 2, p. 72). All the music of Fascicle 2 has been studied and compared; a little more weight has been placed on the older, Toyohara, mouth-organ tradition (KF/HSFRK) when deciding between a number of divergent readings (although this has not been done arbitrarily or in haste); and the melodic line of the conflated version has been influenced by Moronaga's string parts in JCYR, in view of the greater pitch-range available to the zither than to the mouth-organ and bass-lute, at the time when the Japanese sought to preserve this music in written form.

Toraden

Prelude. There is no *Processional* to this suite. The music-and-dance presentation was preceded by the *Modal Prelude* for pieces in the *Ichikotsu-chō* mode-key group. The first movement, the *Prelude,* differs from that of *Ō-dai hajin-raku* in that it is in three sections, each of sixteen drum-beat periods: the first Section unmeasured throughout; the second and third Sections, comprising an alternatively named *Middle Prelude*, each consist of a first measure of five binary-beat units, while the second to the eleventh measures are of four binary units each. Both Sections then proceed '*Prelude*-like' to the end (unmeasured, but quickly, in these two cases). It will be remembered that the *Prelude* of *Ō-dai hajin-raku* is in one complete, unmeasured Section, originally of forty drum-beat periods, but now of thirty. The three Sections of the *Prelude* of *Toraden* together number forty-eight drum-beat periods, of unmeasured and measured music.

In the first drum-beat period of Section 1, the evidence favours a duration of eight beats (the beat is one quarter-note; the binary-beat unit, two quarter-notes) against KF/HSFRK which records six beats. In drum-beat period 5, the conflated version follows KF/HSFRK, JCYR, and SGYR; SSSTF here repeats the notes of the previous sixteen beats, but lengthened to a duration of twenty beats.

Possibly a scribal error, or some other addition, occurred prior to AD 1303, and was redressed later by an adjustment of twelve beats of identifiable formulaic material, spread over drum-beat periods 7 and 8 (addendum (a) in the score, Fascicle 2, p. 20). The parts other than SSSTF and the variant *Prelude* support each other well through the first part of this Section, as do SSSTF and the variant *Prelude,* although the latter *Prelude* has reached the ninth drum-beat, where the other parts mark the eighth. There is evidence here of opposing (or indeed different) traditions among the recorded source materials, and there is further evidence of attempted reconciliation of traditions, in SSSTF, by the compression, later on, of the two drum-beat periods 14 and 15 into one period (the text shows the stave erased at this point). In these two periods, however, the variant *Prelude* agrees with the primary versions of JCYR and SGYR. Addendum (b) has been considered in drum-beat 9, in relation to other sources, and the same applies to (c) (Fascicle 2, p. 22) in drum-beat period 12. There is no difficulty in drum-beat periods 14 and 15, in the light of the firm evidence of the remaining parts (three primary versions and one secondary version).

Section 2 of the *Prelude* begins the *Middle Prelude.* The first measure shows eleven beats in three primary versions and in the variant *Section* (Fascicle 2, pp. 28, 32). The editors have explained that the seventh beat is a mistake. Without it, the correct seventh beat on *c'* introduces the familiar cadence-formula present in both wind parts, and in both versions of the bass-lute parts. This ending has been adopted here, and a ten-beat bar is the result, as in SSSTF. The music now proceeds in measures of eight beats until drum-beat eleven. (d) (Fascicle 2, p. 30) has not been included in period 12 because of the positive agreement between the other parts. Section 3 (the *Middle Prelude,* Section 2) is almost a repetition of the *Prelude,* Section 2; only in the first bar are the notes different. The third and fourth binary units of drum-beat period 12 now include three notes each, an acceptable reading of KF/HSFRK at this point.

Entering Broaching. The *Entering Broaching* shows repetition of the first four measures, as in the score; the original tablature was not written out a second time. After the ninth drum stroke, the direction is given to play in the *Prelude (Jo)*-style. Drum-beat periods 10-12 follow the notation of KF/HSFRK. To accommodate the three notes between the binary-beat markers, a pair of eighth notes has been written, as shown in the string manuscripts; the half-note cadence note has also been supplied in periods 10 and 12. A similar approach has been adopted in drum-beat period 13, where *d'* and *a* are both lengthened. Drum-beat period 14 differs in the parts; and the same variance is evident at this point in the *Stamping* and in the *Quick Tune,* and presumably reflects differing traditions. The clarity and agreement of Moronaga's scores, JCYR and SGYR, leads us to accept the superfinal cadence, although in the first *Stamping* the alternative cadence on the mediant (period 15) is an acceptable and defensible reading.

Stamping. The *Stamping* again yields evidence of traditions fostered independently among wind and string players. The movement is written out once in KF/HSFRK, JCYR and SGYR, with a general direction, at the head of the piece, to play it twice. In SSSTF it is written out twice, and the second time here differs from the first. Is the second version included so as to provide an opportunity for playing the movement the second time, in slightly varied form; or is it intended simply to record the existence of two versions as evidence of alternative performance-traditions, recognized by instrumentalists at the time? Both versions are presented here to show that they existed and to provide a second version for those who wish to make comparison. The eleventh drum-beat marking, in the mouth-organ parts of the first version, has been adopted, as has the thirteenth drum-beat in KF/HSFRK, both of which make musical and structural sense in the light of the more conservative Toyohara-tradition (an important point), and in the light of the readings proposed in this conflation of the remaining periods of the wind parts. The second version in the score shows SSSTF as a new part, with JCYR and SGYR primary versions beneath it. Although more strongly influenced by SSSTF than was the first *Stamping*, as is appropriate in this circumstance, some details of the second conflated version have been decided on under the influence of Moronaga — in particular, his directions for the repetition of periods 3 to 7, and his stronger version of period 14.

Quick Tune. The *Quick Tune* is the same as the *Entering Broaching.* The tablature is complete in all four primary versions; and this time the repeat of the first four measures is written out in full. Apart from the groups of quavers/eighth-notes, only the first note of measure 5 is altered in the repeat. Nevertheless, compared with the *Entering Broaching,* it is the first note of the first measure of the *Quick Tune* that differs. The differences, between periods 10 and 11 of the *Quick Tune* and the same periods of the *Entering Broaching,* are determined here by the primary versions, and by the binary-unit dots of KF/HSFRK. Contrary to KF/HSFRK, however, the antepenultimate cadence is again written on the superfinal, in keeping with a recognizable, quick repeat of the *Entering Broaching* as heard before, but now functioning as the last movement of the ballet suite.

Prelude, **Section 1**

with *taiko*-beats

14   15   16

Prelude, Section 2 – Middle Prelude, Section 1
quick, with *taiko*-beats, and *kakko* as far as *jo*

Prelude, Section 3 – Middle Prelude, Section 2
quick, with *taiko*-beats, and *kakko* as far as *jo*

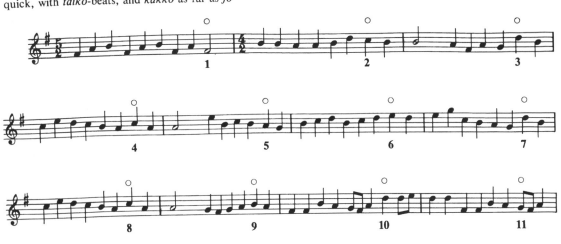

Entering Broaching

play twice (or four times), quickly, with *taiko*-beats, and *kakko* up to *jo*

Stamping

play it twice, quickly, with *taiko*-beats

Seven times quickly, with *taiko*-beats, and *kakko* as far as *jo*

Shunnō-den

Fewer problems arise in reconciling the parts of this suite. The sources are clear, and the extent of agreement is considerable. Sometimes details of rhythm, duration, notes, and repetitions of notes, differ between the parts; but these differences do not seriously affect the nature or quality of the music, nor do they contravene directions in the manuscripts relating to the music and its performance. Solutions to the differences presented here have been reached over a period of time, after careful consideration of alternative possibilities and their implications.

The conflation represents more than the physical form of the music; it attempts also to capture an expression of musical personality in terms defined by the aesthetic standards of the day. The same may be said of the conflations of Ō-dai hajin-raku and Toraden but, because of greater agreement between the primary sources, Shunnō-den reads and runs more confidently. However, in saying this, no reservations about the authenticity of any of these pieces are implied; they are, all three, remarkable and distinctive, both as a genre of music, and as individual items of a performance repertoire.

Processional. There is only one passage in the *Processional* that calls for comment, and that is the reading of the binary units 21-22. All parts agree, in principle, up to this point, but these two binary units show different time-values and rhythms: the mouth-organ sources occupy four beats, as compared with the two beats of the same passages in the string versions. Of the various possibilities at this point (and bearing in mind the fact that the mouth-organ tradition is likely to be the older tradition), the conflation follows SSSTF by retaining the time-structure of the wind parts, and the binary-unit initials of *g″* and *a″*, common to both.

Prelude. In the *Prelude,* KF/HSFRK is usually direct and clear; only minor discrepancies occur, namely, in drum-beat periods 2, 9, and 11. For the first note of period 12, *e″* has been accepted on the strong evidence of parts other than KF/HSFRK.

Stamping and *Entering Broaching.* Except for occasional details of time, rhythm, octave placement, and embellishment, the four sources of the *Stamping* are similar, but independent, records of their several instrumental traditions. KF/HSFRK, a completely legible and musically acceptable part, is again closely endorsed by the other sources. JCYR and SGYR reveal the shapeliness of the extended melodic line. SGYR also provides a secondary version, complete, and free of doubt in the transcription. Decisions in arriving at a conflated version were not difficult. The same can be said of the *Entering Broaching,* where the sources are again straightforward, clean, and complete.

Bird Tune. The conflation of the *Bird Tune* invites two explanatory comments. The first concerns the number of bass-drum strokes. The title, and the directions (four times, very quickly), suggest an imaginative, programmatic instinct on the part of a composer wishing to make a more effective dance-piece out of a very short tune. The part most strongly identified with the call of the Bush Warbler is contained in the last few notes, the repeated binary units: *e″-f♯″* (Fascicle 2, p. 68). JCYR states that nowadays (that is, in the late twelfth century) there are sixteen drum-beats, although none of the parts in the score (when editorial suggestions are removed) conforms to this (Fascicle 2, p. 50). Both SGYR and JCYR (with the three repeats marked in both string parts of the score) indicate twenty *hyaku*; KF/HSFRK, fifteen *hyaku*; and SSSTF, only twelve. The difference in numbers is caused by the absence, in the mouth-organ parts, of directions to repeat the last eight binary-units, and by several omissions of *hyaku* markers earlier in the piece. Moronaga's primary versions are clear and complete in these two respects; the second version in JCYR (dō-kyoku) endorses the repeat of the final eight binary units, but totally omits *hyaku* signs. In making a conflation, one might simply accept a sixteen drum-beat ruling, and amend the omissions from the wind parts, sweeping the string traditions aside. However, none of the sources shows sixteen drum-beats; whereas two, with the final section repeated, show, clearly and indisputably, twenty drum-beats.

In determining an acceptable and convincing version, the decision was made to submit to the authority of Moronaga, and to interpret the prefatory comment to mean that nowadays there are sixteen drum-beats, but earlier there were twenty. Since the aim of members of the Tang Music Project is to get as close as possible to what might have been the original version in China, the twenty *hyaku* markers of JCYR and SGYR have been accepted, and the three repeated sections approved. For these reasons, and contrary to the score, the three repeats have been written out in the conflation for the sake of simplicity and clarity.

The second point for explanation concerns the *a'-f#'-e"* note-sequence at drum-strokes 13 and 17. Attention is drawn to comments in Fascicle 2 which are relevant here; these stress the numerous repetitions, and recognizable pitches, of the reiterated notes e"-f#" in the song of Bush Warblers (Fascicle 2, p. 68). The last eight drum-beat periods and measure equivalents of the *Bird Tune* may indeed be a bird-motif that the composer has deftly incorporated into the closing moments of the piece. Now, with regard to the practicalities of performing these notes,

the mouth-organ has no low *f#'-e'* available in its fixed-pipe tuning system, and consequently has to leap from *a'* up to *f#"-e"* to continue the melody, as written at this point. The zither, however, has both the high and the low F#-E notes in its openstring modal tuning, while the lute has only the lower *f#'-e'* in the idiomatic pitch-range observed in this music. It is interesting to note that, whenever A-F# comes in the first two sections of this movement, it is followed by G, the mouth-organ playing *a'-f#"-g"* and the zither *a'-f#-g* (the same in the bass-lute). After bass-drum stroke 12, however, the melody requires the notes A-F#-E for the first time. The difference in instrumental idiom is now important. The mouth-organ plays what it must, *a'-f#"-e"*, but the zither, which has a choice, sounds the descending third and then leaps up the seventh where *e"-f#"* ring out clearly and brightly from the initial *e"* of the binary unit. The higher notes of the zither are now freed from the modal pedal-points and bass drones, heard so often in the earlier movements, and in the *Bird Tune* until drum-beat 13; the musical effect of these higher notes and their accentual octave doublings must surely have been intentional. The secondary version in JCYR *(dō-kyoku)* also prescribes this manner of performance. The conflation has therefore adopted the striking melodic line approved and demonstrated by Fujiwara no Moronaga. The *Bird Tune*, in 'The Singing of Spring Warblers' finishes, in truth it seems, with the notes of one of Nature's own choicest songsters.

Processional
play several times without *taiko*-beats

Prelude
play twice, with *taiko*-beats

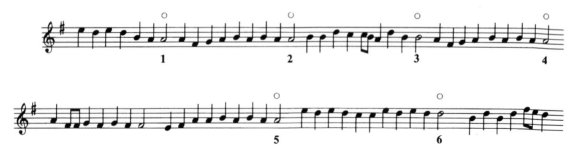

Stamping

play twice, quickly, with *kakko* and *taiko*-beats

Entering Broaching

play four times, quickly, with *kakko* and *taiko*-beats

Bird Tune

play four times, very quickly, with *taiko*-beats

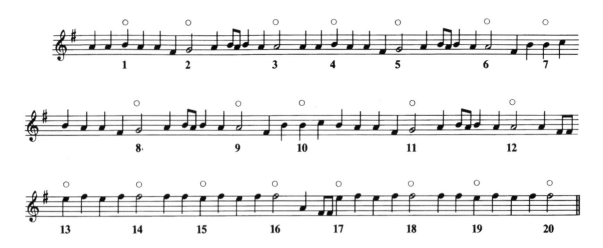

Quick Tune

The same as Entering Broaching — play it twice, quickly

Analytical commentary
on *Toraden* and *Shunnō-den* (N.J.N)

Introduction

The formal, and structural, analytical tables of *Ō-dai hajin-raku* in Fascicle 2 provided evidence of both rational and intuitive organization of musical materials in the composition of that suite. The *Prelude* demonstrated order and grouping, within the thirty drum-beat periods, which could not have been fortuitous. Moreover, there is evidence of both intellectual and musical logic in the structure of the piece, a logic that must have influenced the arrangement of cadence-tones and drum-beat periods into groups, and which saw to it that these groups were placed in relation to each other, so as to express the mode, and so as to satisfy structural requirements within a large-scale composition. Recurrent melodies were identified between the different groups of drum-beat periods of the *Prelude*, and between those of the *Prelude* and the *Broaching*. Evidence was adduced substantiating the view that the manner of composition of *Ō-dai hajin-raku*, was a patchwork assembly of modal formulae, a practice similar to that recognized in medieval chant, both in the East and in the West. Further support for the rational attitudes detected in operation in this suite comes from the historical accounts of the piece.

That the latter part of the *Prelude* was made good after the loss, from memory failure, of dance-movements corresponding to eight drum-beat periods, is fact; and the result of that 'making-good' by the omission of ten drum-beat periods is proof of conscious amendment and considered revision. The music was revised so as to accommodate a musically satisfactory performance of the remainder of the dance (Fascicle 1, pp. 18-20). The nature and degree of revision is not known; but work on the *Prelude* was ordered by the then emperor of Japan, and the result survives to this day in a form which gained acceptance and approval for several centuries, as the primary sources prove. An examination of the two half-Sections of the *Prelude* has shown the independent organization of each: in the first part, on a strong dominant-final structural basis, and in the second part, on a superfinal-final structural basis. Comparison of the two half-Sections clarifies the nature of their differences, and their relationship to each other, as two halves of a reconstructed whole.

With regard to the *Broaching*, similar findings were obtained. The six Sections contain a collection of melodic formulae organized into standard lengths of twenty measures, or measure-equivalents, with drum-beats; and each Section is independent of those on either side of it in its particular perspective on the mode. The recurrent melodic formulae of *Prelude* and *Broaching* are the property of *Ichikotsu-chō*; they embody the note-sets which, when used in this particular way, establish, define, and maintain, the mode in this suite. The manner of discovery of these data was described in Fascicle 2, pp. 74–99. But although formulae common to both movements were recognized, no evidence was forthcoming to justify an assumption that the *Prelude* was composed before the *Broaching*, or *vice versa*. Examination of *Toraden* and *Shunnō-den* now enables us to take matters a stage further.

Toraden

In the score of *Toraden*, there are four movements comprising a total of six Sections; with repeats of Sections made as directed in the texts, at least fourteen Sections will be counted during performance, when the work is played in full. Putting aside the numbers of repeats of the Sections, it would seem at first sight that the suite comprises only four distinct compositions, since Section 3 of the *Prelude* repeats Section 2 (Sections 2 and 3 make the *Middle Prelude*), and the *Quick Tune* is the same as the *Entering Broaching*. Even so, a closer look at the various Sections and movements, reveals that all are, in fact, variants of each other.

A Table displaying the three Sections of the *Prelude* shows that, following the first measure (or measure equivalent) of each, Section 2 is a shadow of Section 1, and Section 3 an even closer copy of Section 2. The differences between Sections primarily concern time and rhythm; the degree of melodic divergence is rudimentary and inconsequential. In this study, it is unnecessary to consider whether any of these differences were originally intended, or whether they were acquired as a result of later, idiomatic, instrumental practices introduced and perpetuated by the authority of family or courtly traditions.

TABLE 1. Sections 1, 2 and 3 of the *Prelude*

Attention is drawn to the measures of ten beats with which Sections 2 and 3 of the *Prelude* (that is, the two parts of the *Middle Prelude*) begin. It is feasible to interpret the rhythmic grouping of these measures as: 3 + 3 + 2 + 2. Among the scores of Section 2, SSSTF is the only one to show ten beats; the total of eleven beats shown by other parts is unacceptable, given the established principle of the use of binary units as building-cells. Even so, the binary-beat markers in SSSTF (ᵒ) appear to be misplaced, or faultily transcribed, at source. Fortunately, the first measure of Section 3 is less variable. All parts agree on ten beats, and the idiomatic, instrumental style of the zither part (JCYR) supports an internal rhythmic structure of 3 + 3 + 2 + 2, independent of the binary unit insisted upon at other times. The markers in SSSTF indicate the first, fourth, and seventh, notes as group-initials, although not (apparently in this case) marking binary units as might have been expected. The full explanation of this last point remains elusive. Could there be some particular physical movement and musical significance in the triple formula *f#'-a'-b'* heard in the opening phrases of all three Sections of this movement? (see the discussion of this point in Fascicle 2, p. 27). The opening drum-beat period of the first Section introduces the motif of these three notes in a prominent binary-unit statement.

What is clear and supportable about the first period or measure is this: that the problem, if indeed it is a problem, does not apply to Section 1, since the binary-unit markings there are in agreement in all parts; that the fourth notes of Sections 2 and 3, in three of the primary sources, indicate the initial of a beat-group and the completion of the previous beat-group; that the seventh and ninth notes of SSSTF, in Section 2, also have these indications (the sixth, eighth, and tenth, notes of KF/HSFRK are worth comparing with it in this regard); that the seventh notes in the score of Section 3, in the same three sources, have the same indicators;

and that the zither strengthens the ninth beat of this measure in the same way as it does the fourth and seventh beats of the same measure. Apart from questions of rhythmic structure, the formula *f#'-a'-b'* can be regarded analytically as structurally significant, because the opening measure, or measure-equivalent, of each of the three Sections, although individually different phrases, all feature it prominently. While recognizing the possibility of its having some functional importance, it will be noticed that the note-formula is little used elsewhere. There is one further observation: the cadence-formula on *e*, at the end of period 4 of Section 1, does not occur in the following Sections of the *Prelude*, although it is represented in later movements of the suite on drum beats 9 and 14 (except in several sources for the first *Stamping*).

TABLE 2. The *Entering Broaching*, the *Stamping* and the *Quick Tune*

1   In the score, the repeat of the *Quick Tune* is written out in full. In the conflation, the repeat shows three small differences from the first four measures.

80

Entering Broaching

It is evident that the six pieces are very closely related. All the openings differ, though there is a common identity, in the use of the formula *f#'-a'-b'*, among four of them, and an even closer resemblance (but without the formula) between the remaining two. The first four drum-beat periods, or measures, of all the parts are the least stable in comparative analysis; but the basic outlines can easily be traced through all the parts. It is the nature and degree of rhythmic independence between the six staves that is musically significant. Not only is the barring system different in the early segments of the pieces, but the tempo and rhythmic organization also differ (and not only in the first measures of Sections 2 and 3 of the *Prelude*, discussed above).

It will be seen also that repetition of the first four measures or drum-beat periods, of the *Entering Broaching*, the *Stamping*, and the *Quick Tune*, in fact covers twice the amount of musical time as do the comparable periods or measures of the Sections of the *Prelude*. The last include no formal repeats; but the return of certain drum-beat periods is evident: much of periods 4 and 7; all of periods 5 and 8; periods 9 and 12; and periods 10 and 11. From period 12 onwards, the six parts imitate each other closely to the end.

Is there evidence, in this comparative table of all the pieces of *Toraden*, on which to base an opinion whether there is a 'main tune' from which all the others derive? It could be argued that the measured *Entering Broaching* and *Quick Tune* are self-contained, in four subdivisions of four measures, each tidily balanced and well ordered, the repeated measures strengthening the case for musical planning and conscious management of musical ideas. It could

also be argued, however, that the free, unmeasured Section 1 of the *Prelude* expresses the original ideas, subsequently subjected to regular metre and with added preludial codas, according to dance traditions and functional requirements of this kind of entertainment. There is no case as yet for consideration of a theme-and-variations principle, or for a protomelody from which all movements derive. It will be noted, however, that the arguments put forward in regard to *Entering Broaching* and *Quick Tune* support the suggestion, made in Fascicle 2 (see p. 100), that the *Entering Broaching*, perhaps, was the original nucleus out of which the suite was developed.

Comparison of the remaining movements of *Toraden* is similarly enlightening. It is the *first Stamping* that appears in the Table, and measures 5-8 of the *Quick Tune* are here contained in the repeat sign. After the opening, the identity of each piece is revealed. The form is the same. The first measures of the *Entering Broaching* and the *Quick Tune* adopt the dominant cadence-formula, familiar from the beginning of the second section of the *Prelude*; while the *Stamping* adopts the submediant cadence-formula from the first Section of the *Prelude*. From the ninth measure onwards, the parts (*Entering Broaching, Stamping, Quick Tune*) compare very closely. In the fifteenth measure of the *Stamping*, the first reading of the conflation is shown. It will be remembered that two traditions are evident in the three movements at this point: the Toyohara family tradition consistently writes the mediant, while Moronaga, just as consistently, writes the superfinal.

It now remains to view the six separate staves in simultaneous alignment.

TABLE 3 The *Prelude* (in three Sections), the *Entering Broaching,* the *Stamping,* and the *Quick Tune*

Shunnō-den

The suite *Shunnō-den* is in six movements: *Processional, Prelude, Stamping, Entering Broaching, Bird Tune,* and *Quick Tune.* As the *Processional* is part of the *Prelude,* and the *Quick Tune* a repeat of the *Entering Broaching,* there are in fact only four different piece to consider: *Prelude, Stamping, Entering Broaching* and *Bird Tune.*

In the *Prelude* there are repetitions and variant-repetitions of drum-beat periods, as in the other two suites in *Ichikotsu-chō.* Periods that are the same are: 2 and 4; 5 and 13; 6, 8, 14 and 16; and 7 and 15. Partial resemblances are also present: 5 and 13 are extended versions of 2 and 4; the four final binary units of period 11 are cadence-material in periods 7 and 15; and most of period 10 is extended in period 12. Structurally, the movement consists of groups of four drum-beat periods, of which the second group, periods 5-8, is repeated in the fourth group, periods 13-16, making an **ABCB** form. Drum-beat periods 5-8 supply the music for the *Processional.*

The *Stamping* (also known as *Middle Prelude*) is constructed similary to the *Prelude:* periods 2 and 4 are almost the same; while 5 and 13; 6, 8, 14, and 16; and 7 and 15; are the same. Close resemblances exist between periods 5, 7, and 15. The formal design is again **ABCB**, where **C** demonstrates a different aspect of the mode from that in **A** and **B**. The difference lies in the hexachord *g'-a'-b'-c"-d"-e"*, where the first two measures of **C** (9 and 10) establish an order of notes by weighting-formula, strongest to weakest: d, b, c, **a**, g, e.[1] In the next two measures (11 and 12), this changes to *b', **a'**, c", g', e",* from which the final is absent. The dominant is the cadence-note in both cases (Fascicle 2, p. 60, and Tables 4 and 5) Both the subdominant

and the subfinal are the least heard notes in **A** and **B**, that is, in measures 1-8, where the subfinal occurs only once. In measures 9-12, the subfinal, in particular, is more important.

The same number of drum-beat periods is heard in the *Entering Broaching* as in the *Stamping.* Variants of periods 7 and 15 are to be found in periods 5 and 13; and variants of periods 3 and 4 in periods 11 and 12, respectively. **ABCB** is again the form of the movement.

Several different aspects of the mode are further demonstrated. The table below shows the comparative weight of each note of the scale of the mode, in each group of four measures, from the strongest to the weakest, moving left to right across the page (cadence-note in bold type).

TABLE 4. Order of note-weighting in the *Entering Broaching*

	measures					
A,	1- 4,	**a'**	d"	b'	e"	f# = g
B,	5- 8,	f#	**d**	a	b	e
C,	9-10,	c	d	**a** = b	c	
	11-12,	**a**	d	f#	b	
B,	13-16,	f#	**d**	a	b	e

The shortest movement in the score is the *Bird Tune;* but with its three repeats written out, as in the conflation, it measures up to the *Stamping* and the *Entering Broaching: Stamping,* 64 binary units with 16 drum-beats; *Entering Broaching,* 48 binary units with 16 drum-beats; *Bird Tune,* 46 binary units with 20 drum-beats; and *Quick Tune* (the same as the *Entering Broaching*), 48 binary units with 16 drum-beats. Repeating phrases of the *Bird Tune* (not drum-beat periods, in this case), marked off by half-note cadences, are phrases 1 and 3; phrases 2, 4, 6 and 8; phrases 5 and 7;

1 Cadence-note bold.

86

and phrases 9, 10, 11, and 12. The scale of the tune is *e'-f#'-g'-a'-b'-c"*; the concluding cadence is on *f#"*, and the final of the *Ichikotsu-chō* mode-key (D) is not sounded in the *Bird Tune*. The weighted-scale of the complete melody shows that, in the absence of the final of the mode, the dominant and mediant of the *Ichikotsu-chō* modal-classi-fication weigh more than double the weight of any other individual note of the piece, in this order:

a (74), f# (62), b (30), e = g (16), and c (4),

(see Fascicle 2, p. 67, and Tables 4 and 5) although, like the dominant and mediant, the subdominant plays an impor-tant role as a cadence-note, which allots to it somewhat particular prominence. The form is: **A A A₁ A₁ B B.** A comparative table of the four movements displays their common identity, and the musical language of the suite.

TABLE 5. *Prelude, Stamping, Entering Broaching* **and** *Bird Tune*

15/19   16/20

(Prelude)

(Stamping)

(Entering Broaching)

Comparison between movements is instructive. Of particular interest is the similarity between them in periods 1-5, since this is where the *Bird Tune* reveals most clearly its connections in musical thought with the other movements. In periods 9-10 and 13-14 again there is a recognizable outline shared between the parts. The *Prelude* and the *Stamping* lie quite close together for nine of the sixteen drum-beat periods, but period 6 is distinctive in each part, although a prototype cadential formula can be discerned in both. The *Entering Broaching* shares this cadence form with the *Stamping* in this measure, and this reciprocity recurs in measures 8, 14, and 16. *Prelude* and *Entering Broaching* also reflect each other in nine of the drum-beat periods; and, aided by the similarity of the recurrent measures 6, 8, 14 and 16, and the regular metres, the *Stamping* reflects the *Entering Broaching*, or *vice versa*, in twelve of its sixteen measures.

One may safely infer, from the historical accounts, that the *Bird Tune* was the elegant and effective reply to an imperial command to capture in musical terms the singing of the warblers at dawn in the spring (see Fascicle 2, p. 45). If this was the case, one may also infer that the *Bird Tune* might well have been the inspiration for other movements added later. The imperial command, for a composition inspired by the experience and delight of that morning, produced a certain musical response from a musician of the court (Fascicle 2, p. 45). What is more probable than that a composer, close to the emperor,

seeking his approbation and favour, would make more music on the same natural and musical themes of the original composition? As shown here, the data from analysis are compatible with such a view of the manner of generation of this suite from an original nucleus, imitative of a specific bird-song.

The simultaneous comparison of the movements of these suites strengthens opinions reached and presented in Fascicle 2, in the discussion of the music of *Ō-dai hajin-raku*. The language of this music comprises a miscellany of melodic formulae which the musician, thinking creatively, assembled intuitively from formulae familiar to his imagination, common to his performance medium, and embedded in the musical style of the day. Manipulation and management of these formulae created measured and unmeasured pieces of music for dance entertainment, of which tempi, phrase-structure and performance-characteristics, were variable and flexible.

The patchwork process is thus endorsed in *Toraden* and *Shunnō-den,* as it was in *Ō-dai hajin-raku*. Although common formulae are recognizable in all three works, there are also groups of formulae peculiar to each suite. The manner of composition is that of a folk style, popular entertainment music, for ballets at the Chinese court. Each of the suites has a characteristic melodic personality, defined by the common mode, and by contemporary standards of musicality and craftsmanship.

Mouth-organ techniques in the Song and Ming Dynasties

The sounding of other notes, along with the melody-note, in mouth-organ performance in China, and a possible aural stimulus to the development, by the Japanese, of cluster-chords (*aitake* 合竹).

In search of information regarding mouth-organ (*sheng*) performance in China during the period of Japanese borrowing of music from the Tang Court, our attention has been drawn to descriptions of the *sheng* in works of the Song and Ming Dynasties, no such Chinese description being known for the Tang period.[1] In a recent study, Professor Yang Yinliu 楊蔭劉 has set out the data, summarized in a passage from the Song *Yueshu* (j. 123), both in tabular form and in staff-notation on bass and treble staves. These data relate to three sizes of mouth-organs, overlapping in compass, each consisting of nineteen free-reed pipes. For each of the pipes of the instrument that cover the middle pitch-range, the Song text states, in sequence from 1 to 19, the serial number, the individual name, the absolute pitch and octave, and the serial number of what is termed the 'responding' pipe.[2] This last is either the lower or the upper octave of the note yielded by a pipe of given serial number. Some pipes are said to have 'no responding pipe'. The notes with responding pipes are those of the Chinese basic, Lydian, heptatonic scale: F G A B C D E; the intermediate semitone degrees: F# G# A# C# D#, have no upper or lower octave in the set of nineteen pipes.

Although no consonance other than the octave is specified in this Song account (the text and translation are shown in Plate 3), it is certain from Ming sources, and from Zhu Zaiyu 朱載堉 in particular, that octaves and fifths were sounded simultaneously with the melody note. The example given is: lower-octave (倍) *Huangzhong* (*F*) is sounded with middle-range (正) *Huangzhong* (*f*), with lower-octave *Linzhong* 林鐘倍律 (*C*), and with middle-range *Linzhong* 林鐘正律 (*c*); the thumb and first finger of the left hand, and the middle and first finger of the right

hand close four holes, one in each of four pipes, thus increasing the impedance of those pipes and forcing the reed to speak when the wind-pressure increases. (The full text is shown in Plate 4, along with a translation of the passage.)[3]

This example suggests that, in the Ming Dynasty, and in the practice of the Confucian ritual orchestra, octaves, and the fifth with its octave, were still the only notes sounded together with a given melody-note. The same chapter of the *Yueshu*, namely j. 123, contains further information, however, on the intervallic distance between the corresponding pipes of three sizes of *sheng*[4]: *yusheng* 竽笙, *chaosheng* 巢笙, and *hesheng* 合笙 (Plate 5). Given the fact that the intervallic relationship between the pipes in the numerical sequence 1 – 19 was the same for the three different sizes, Professor Yang demonstrates that the *sheng* of lowest pitch (the *yu*) lay at an interval of a sixth (nine semitone degrees = nine *liu* 律) below the *sheng* of middle range (the *chao*); while the *sheng* of highest pitch (the *he*), lay at an interval of a fourth (five semitone degrees) above the *sheng* of middle-range.

The central portion of the gamut of each *sheng* was a complete chromatic octave, referred to as 'the twelve proper notes' 十二正聲 At the lower end, below this set, there were 'three muddy notes' 三濁聲 (that is, low notes) separated from the first note of the chromatic octave by the interval of a tritone. At the upper end, above the complete chromatic octave, there were 'four clear notes' 四清聲 (high notes) at intervals of fifth, tone, and tone. The diagram that follows on p. 96 is a simplified version of that given by Yang Yinliu.

1 We are indebted to Professor Li Chunyi 李純一 , and Dr Tong Kinwoon, 唐健垣 , for references to the *Yueshu* 樂書 of Chen Yang 陳暘 (1101), and to the *Lulu-jingyi neibian* of Zhu Zaiyu, and it was Dr Tong who drew our attention to the recent work of Professor Yang Yinliu: *Zhongguo gudai yinyue shigao* 中國古代音樂史稿 (A draft history of ancient Chinese music) (1980) Renmin Yinyue chubanshe, *shang-ce*, pp. 367-71.

2 *Yueshu*, j. 123, pp. 3b, 4a. The important data on 'responding' notes are contained in the commentary in smaller type. The edition used is that printed in Canton in 1876. (University Library, Cambridge, Photographic Department)

3 *Lulu jingyi neibian*, j. 18, 'Method of playing large and small *yu*-mouth-organs' *Dayu, xiaoyu chuifa* 大竽小竽吹法 (Photograph of the original text in a copy of the first edition, University Library, Cambridge. Photograph by the Photographic Department of the University Library.)

4 *Yueshu*, j. 123, p. 4b. The data on the relationship between the three sizes of mouth-organ – *yu, chao,* and *he* – begin in the fifth column, counting the chapter heading as 1, with the personal name Ruan Yi 阮逸 . (University Library, Cambridge, Photographic Department)

Since the pipes of all three sizes of mouth-organ were named in the same way, and disposed in the same sequence, it is conceivable that the three sizes were at times played together. Three players, simultaneously playing the same tune, using identical fingering on the three different sizes, each accompanying the melody-note with octaves and fifths, would collectively generate a harmonious ensemble of cluster-chords (123.56), moving in parallel with each note of the melody.

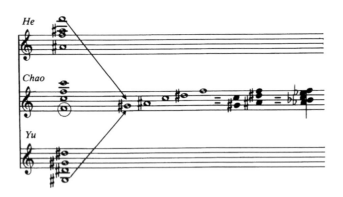

While it is convenient to represent this chord by figures in this order, the particular inversion, and the distribution of the notes in musical space, would differ with each melody-note. Unlike the *aitake* 合竹 ('harmonious bamboos') of current Japanese practice, these cluster-chords would have been variants of a single chord, changing only in the distribution of the same constituent notes over four octaves.

This is, of course, speculation; but the advantage of constructing three sizes of mouth-organs, all pitched within the compass of a ninth, has otherwise no explanation.

As listed in the famous study of the surviving instruments in the Japanese National Treasure-House (*Shōsō-in*) (*Shōsō-in no gakki* 正倉院の樂器 , Tokyo 1967), all the surviving *shō* of Tang date are termed *u/yu* 竽, the name of the bass-*sheng* described in the *Yueshu*; but none of these instruments has more than 17 pipes, and the names written on the pipes are the tablature-signs of *shō*-notations, *not* the absolute-pitch names of the Ming sources or the names, *sui generis,* of the Song *Yueshu*. The surviving artefacts themselves do not, therefore, support the suggestion that the Japanese knew a *shō* of 19 pipes, still less, that they knew three different sizes of such a *shō*. Of the ten cluster-chords in use today on the *shō*, one is a 123.56 chord in root-position, while four are inversions of this in various positions: first, fourth, and sixth.

聖朝李照作巢笙合二十四聲以應律呂正倍之聲作
和笙應笙竽合清濁之聲又自制大笙上之太樂亦可
謂知復古制矣今太常笙濁聲十二中聲十二清聲十
二俗呼為鳳笙孟蜀主所進樂工不能吹雖存而不用
比者按習清濁正三倍聲皆得相應誠去四清聲吹之
雖用之雅樂亦惡在其為不可哉

今巢笙之制
第一管頭子應鐘清聲應第三管
第二中音黃鐘清聲應中音子
第三管應鐘中聲應頭子
第四管南呂中聲應帝五子
第五中呂管無射清聲無應
第六大托管蕤賓濁聲應托聲
第七十五管大呂清聲無應
第八大韻管姑洗濁聲有應
第九帝五子南呂清聲應第四管
第十中音子黃鐘中聲應中音
十一托聲管蕤賓清聲應大托
十二著聲子姑洗清聲應大韻
十三弦呂管夾鐘正聲無應
十四高聲管太簇清聲應后韻
十五平調子林鐘清聲
十六平調管林鐘中聲
十七后韻太簇正聲應高聲
十八義聲管夷則正聲無應十
九托聲管仲呂正聲無應聲

鳳笙

和笙

傳曰大笙音聲眾而高也小者音相和也斯不亦笙大
小之辨乎說文曰笙正月之音十三簧象鳳身蓋其簧

Plate 3   The original text, on which Yang Yinliu's table and notation are based, is shown here in smaller lexigraphs, beginning in the sixth column from the right. The plate reproduces pages 3b and 4a from Chapter 123 of the *Yueshu* (*c.* 1101) (Canton edn of 1876). The woodcut on the left shows, schematically, 'the harmonious mouth-organ' *he-sheng* or 'the roc (mythical bird) mouth-organ' *feng-sheng*.

'In the Chao [if this is the name of an ancient state, it should be read Zhao] mouth-organ as made today, the first pipe *(touzi)*, *e‴*, is the respondent to the third pipe. [The text has 'second', but Yang Yinliu corrects to 'third'.] (2) *(zhongyin)*, *f′*, is the respondent to *zhongyinzi*. The third pipe, *e″*, is the respondent to *touzi* [*e‴*]. The fourth pipe, *d″*, is the respondent to *diwuzi*. (5) the *zhonglu*-pipe, *d#′*, has no respondent. (6) the *datuo*-pipe, *b*, is the respondent to *tuosheng*. (7) the 'fifteenth-pipe *shiwuguan, f#′*, has no respondent. [The text wrongly has 鍾 in place of 無 .] (8) the *dayun*-pipe, *a,* has a respondent. [Yang Yinliu observes that the text should read 'is the respondent to the *zhushengguan*.' The Canton edition reads: 有唐元　　– presumably a corruption of 有應。九 ...] (9) *diwuzi, d‴* is the respondent to the fourth pipe [*d″*] [Here 鍾 should read 第 .] (10) *zhongyinzi, f″*, is the respondent to *zhongyin* [*f′*]. (11) the *tuosheng*-pipe, *b′*, is the respondent to *datuo* [*b*]. (12) the *zhusheng*-pipe, *a′,* is the respondent to *dayun* [*a*]. (13) the *zhonglu*-pipe. *g#*, has no respondent. (14) the *gaosheng*-pipe, *g′*, ['is the respondent to *houyun, g'* – omitted from the text.] (15) *pingdiaozi, c‴* [correcting *linzhong zhengsheng* to *linzhong qingsheng*; 'is the respondent' is here omitted, since the next pipe is the responding pipe.] (16) the *pingdiao*-pipe, *c″*. (17) *houyun* [correcting 大 to 后], *g*, is the respondent to *gaosheng* [*g′*]. (18) the *yisheng*-pipe, *c#″*, has no respondent. (19) the *tuosheng*-pipe, *a#′*, has no respondent.'

The translation converts all the pitchpipe-names to pitches, supposing that *huangzhong* is *f*. All the individual names of the pipes are transliterated, so that the fact that these are *sui generis*, unrelated to any other system of pitch-notation, is displayed.

The sequence of pitches (descending) is shown here with the serial numbers of the pipes written above, and ringed:

①　⑨　⑮　⑩　③　⑤　④　⑱　⑯　⑪　⑲　⑫　⑬　⑭　⑦　②　⑥　⑧　⑰
e‴　d‴　c‴　f′　e″　d#′　d″　c#″　c″　b′　a#′　a′　g#′　g′　f#′　f′　b　a　g

In numerical sequence then, the successive pitches yielded by the pipes are:

①　②　③　④　⑤　⑥　⑦　⑧　⑨　⑩　⑪　⑫　⑬　⑭　⑮　⑯　⑰　⑱　⑲
e‴　f′　e″　d″　d#′　b　f#′　a　d‴　f″　b′　a′　g#　g′　c‴　c″　c#″　a#′

This at first sight surprising sequence is determined by considerations of convenience in fingering pipes, simultaneously, with (for example) thumb and first finger of the left hand, and middle and first fingers of the right hand, closing lower venting-holes, to obtain a chord of a fifth, with each note doubled at the octave – say, *a a′ e″ e‴*.

The names of the set of 19 pipes, the same for three different sizes of mouth-organ, are:

① *touzi* ② *zhongyin* ③ *disanguan* ④ *disiguan* ⑤ *zhongluguan* ⑥ *dutuoguan* ⑦ *shiwuguan* ⑧ *dayunguan* ⑨ *diwuzi* ⑩ *zhongyinzi* ⑪ *tuoshengguan* ⑫ *zhushengguan* ⑬ *xianluguan* ⑭ *gaoshengguan* ⑮ *pingdiaozi* ⑯ *pingdiaoguan* ⑰ *houyun* ⑱ *yishengguan* ⑲ *tuoshengguan*.

93

十三簧為小笙　有正無倍　是名小笙

爾雅曰笙小者謂之和註云十三簧者即此器也其十二簧

為六律六呂之正聲其一簧為黃鍾之半聲夫黃鍾正聲已

具於六律之中矣又有半聲何也不如此則無以見其循環

無端之妙也是以十二律外多一簧以象閏所謂閏餘魠者

是也古人律準十三弦和笙十三簧其義一也

大竽小竽吹法

每管外面各刻律名正倍字樣假如其簧是黃看何孔上所

刻有黃鍾倍律四字者左于大指按之有黃鍾正律四字者

左手食指按之有林鍾倍律四字者左于中指按之有林鍾

正律四字者右手食指按之四簧齊鳴總是一箇黃字待琴

瑟彈操縵兩段皆畢方繞換手餘律放此

Plate 4　　p. 34b from the fourth volume of Prince Zhu Zaiyu's *Lulu jingyi neibian* j. 18, carries entries on two topics: 'The small mouth-organ *(xiao-sheng)* of 13 free-reeds' (right-hand heading) and 'Method of blowing [= playing] large *yu* and small *yu*'. (*Yu* was the name for mouth-organs with 19 pipes.) (central heading) The text reads: 'On the outside of each pipe is carved the pitchpipe-name and the lexigraphs *zheng* [= proper] or *bei* [= doubled – that is, a pipe of twice the length, sounding the lower octave], for example. If its score is [= shows] *huang*, look to see above which [pipe-] hole the four lexigraphs: *Huangzhong beilu* (f′), are carved, and press it [the hole] with the thumb of the left hand. On the one with the four lexigraphs: *Huangzhong zhenglu (f″),* press it [the hole] with the first finger of the left hand. On the one with the four lexigraphs: *Linzhong beilu (c″),* press it [the hole] with the middle finger of the right hand. On the one with the four lexigraphs: *Linzhong zhenglu (c‴),* press it [the hole] with the first finger of the right hand. The four reeds sound uniformly.'

This plate reproduces the text of the original Ming print of *c.* 1606 (see Kuttner p. 166).

94

十二以應十二律也其一以象閏也

聖朝登歌用和笙取其大者倡則小者和非阮逸所謂

取其聲清和也用十三簧非阮逸所謂十九簧也巢和

若均用十九簧何以辨小大之器哉阮逸謂竽笙起第

四管為黃鍾巢笙起中音管為黃鍾和笙起平調子為黃

鍾各十九簧皆有四清聲三濁聲十二正聲以編鍾四

清聲參驗則和笙平調子是黃鍾清也竽笙第五子是

太簇清也中呂管是大呂清也中音子是夾鍾清也既

已謂之竽矣謂之笙矣安得合而一之為竽笙邪儀禮

所謂三笙一和者不過四人相為倡和孰謂竽和之

Plate 5   p. 4b from the *Yueshu*, j. 123. The data relating named pipes with their pitches for different sizes of *sheng* are quoted from Ruan Yi 阮逸 , a Song Dynasty scholar, active in the eleventh century, author of a collection of essays on topics in the ritual music, and of works on instruments in the Confucian orchestra. Reading from his name in the fourth column we have: 'Ruan Yi states: "On the *yusheng*, starting with the *disiguan* [– pipe], one makes *f*'; on the *chaosheng*, starting with the *zhongyin* [-pipe], one makes *f*'; on the *hesheng*, starting with the *pingdiao* [-pipe], one makes *f"*. As to each set of 19 reeds, in each there are four 'clear' notes, three 'muddy' notes, and 12 'proper' notes." '

Since the fourth pipe on the *yusheng* yields *f*', but on the *chaosheng* (see data set out in Plate 3), *d"*, the former mouth-organ must be pitched a sixth (that is nine semitone-degrees = *lu* 律) below the latter; and since the fifteenth pipe on the *hesheng* yields *f"'*, but *c"'* on the *chaosheng* (Plate 3), the former must be pitched a fourth (that is five semitone-degrees *lu*) above the latter.

New insights since the publication of Fascicle 1 (1981)

(1) The principal bass-drum stroke at the ends of drum-beat periods, in *senza-misura, tempo-giusto Preludes,* is to be played with the note on which the period cadences. The method of notation of this drum-stroke: *hyaku* 百 , following the tablature sign for the note, but written to the right of the central axis of the column of tablature signs in the string parts, must date from a period anterior to the year 966 in which Minamoto no Hiromasa (Hakuga) edited his collection of flute scores (*Hakuga no fue-fu*) (Marett 1976). In Hakuga's work, this mode of mensural notation survives only in two Sections of a single *Prelude* (Marett's System V); elsewhere (Systems I to IV, and other movements in System V) Hakuga's mensural notation has assumed its later, general style, with *hyaku* written to the right of the note on which a drum-beat falls. The retention of this archaic method of notation suggests, perhaps, that *senza-misura, tempo-giusto* Preludes were among the first movements of suites to cease to be performed, and even that they ceased to be performed, in some instances at least, in the Heian period and during Moronaga's lifetime. In the light of Marett's analysis of the six systems of notation, scrupulously reflected in Hakuga's compilation, a latest possible date can only be associated with a single system (IV); but the observed sequence of teachers and performers specified in Hakuga's colophon extends backwards into the eighth century; and the distinctive practice of mensural notation displayed in such *Preludes* might well be not later than the Jōwa period (承和) (834-47) when the *Prelude* of *Ō-dai hajin-raku* was deliberately truncated, and its definitive dimensions determined (Fascicle 1, p. 18).

That *Ō-dai hajin-raku* belongs to the group of items from the *Tōgaku*-repertory which ceased to be performed at a very early date is suggested by a passage in the KKCMJ (Eckhardt 1956). References to performances of *Tōgaku*-pieces in that compilation extend in time from the beginning of the tenth century (924) to the late twelfth century (1178), yet during that interval no full performance of *Ō-dai* is clearly recorded. The only reference to the suite is a statement that, in the time of Horikawa-in, at a festival in the first month, the emperor himself 'began to play [= blow] the piece at the 'low-table shelter' at the time of the 'standing music'. It is not certain, however, that the piece was then played in its entirety. (See Eckardt for details.)

(2) It is plain from the usage of *Gakkaroku 29* (Fascicle 2, p. 48), that the term *kotoba/ci* 詞 (in Chinese a type of lyric-form, as well as 'words'; in Japanese 'words', the *on*-reading being used for 'poetry') may also mean 'notes'. Eckardt, in translating RMS on the stamping of *Shunnō-den,* reads *kotoba* as *kakko*-beats (*Untertakte der Kakko*). Context shows, however, that the meaning is 'notes' associated with time-units of the duration of a *kakko*-beat; and, as the passage from GKR *29* confirms, *kotoba* is a

meaningful term, even in the absence of strokes on the *kakko*-drum. *Kotoba* are evidently 'notes' in the sense of a sound of defined duration, rather than mere pitches.

Conclusive evidence that *kotoba* meant 'notes' in the thirteenth century is afforded by the KKS text (*maki dai* 1, p. 28, Nihon Shisō Taikei edn) in reference to the musical text of the *Rin'yū-ranjō* (see p. 48): 'its notes tell' *sore no kotoba un* 其詞云 — preceding the flute tablature of this *ranjō*.

(3) Again, from the use of 'piece' (*kyoku* 曲) in the statement (Fascicle 2, p. 13): 'the second Section of the *Middle Prelude* is the secret *Section* of the said *piece*', it was evidently possible to use this word for a part of a single movement, or for a complete single movement, of a piece consisting of several movements. In the light of this usage, Tokimoto's comment on the possibly heterogeneous nature of the *Broaching* of *Ō-dai hajin-raku* becomes more comprehensible (Fascicle 1, p. 77). He is stating that Tokimoto's *Broaching* inherited other, in the sense of different, Sections (*takyoku* 他曲).

(4) Attention may be drawn to the weight that may properly be attached, in the light of our accumulated observations, to the mouth-organ parts when attempting to decide what was the original condition of the musical line. Of all parts available to us, the mouth-organ part – and in particular KF/HSFRK (of 1201 at the latest) – presents us with minimally decorated versions of Tang originals.

(5) It is important to distinguish between the terms 'music-beats' (*gakubyōshi* 樂拍子 ; Fascicle 1, p. 10) and 'music blowing' (*gaku-fuku* 樂吹 ; this fascicle p. 9). The former is used for a type of syncopated decoration: the latter is used in the sense of *misurato* – 'measured' – as opposed to *senza-misura, tempo-giusto*. It implies use of the *kakko*-drum and, generally speaking, a faster pace than *jo-fuku* 序吹 '*Prelude*-blowing'. In the preface from KCF to 'A Jade Tree's Rear-Court Blossom', 'music-blowing' is plainly used in contrast to '*Prelude*-blowing'; and here the distinction between the two can only reside (a) in the presence or absence of a percussion stroke associated with each note – the beat of the *kakko* – and (b) in pace.

Whatever primary meaning the term *komebyōshi/long-paizi* 籠拍子 may once have had, its usage seems to be to describe the metrical condition in which, in a measured piece, the measures may be of at least two different lengths – for example, $\frac{3}{2}$ and $\frac{4}{2}$ (see Fascicle 1, p. 65).

(6) Support for the view expressed in Fascicle 1 (p. 56) that the practice of the emperor himself, and of the nobility, is preserved in the glosses ascribed to 'Horikawa-in' in JCYR and SGYR, is given by the passage in the KKCMJ already referred to under (1). The Emperor is said to have begun 'to blow *Ō-dai* – a beautiful and unusual event'. The cautious author, Tachibana Narisue, adds, however, that

the statement that the then Chancellor of the Right (*Ufu* 右府) reported this event, requires investigation.

(7) With the completion of Fascicle 3, it has become evident that, although the total number of what the Chinese called 'large pieces' 大曲 *daikyoku/daqu* included in the repertory of *Tōgaku*, as preserved in *Jinchi-yōroku* and *Sango-yōroku*, is small, perhaps no more than eight in all, a much higher proportion than had hitherto been suspected of the items that now survive as single movements in the modern repertory were still small suites of three movements in the late Heian period, or were known at that time to have been such in the recent past. It is of importance that these three-movement suites embody the *Prelude, Broaching,* and *Quick* type of structure (序 , 破 , 急 , *Jo, Ha, Kyū/Xu, Po, Ji*) which was transmuted into a general aesthetic principle of design in temporal sequence, in the writings of Zeami (with his father the virtual creator of *Nō*) in the early fifteenth century. The evidence for conscious assembly of unrelated movements in the construction of *Katen* (p. 20) provides an item of particular potential interest from the standpoint of modal analysis, and as material for an examination of the respective musical languages of 'Tang' and 'Japanese' melodies of the Heian period.

(8) N.J.N. recently (15 January 1983) suggested that, possibly, the music itself of the *Prelude* of O-dai was not, in fact, shortened, but that, literally, eight *taiko*-strokes were omitted. This would account for the observed greater length of individual drum-beat periods in the latter half of the *Prelude*. Since, however, it was a *dancer* who had forgotten the (last) eight drum-beats, it is reasonable to suppose that it was indeed a portion of the *dance* that had been forgotten, and not the mere placing of eight *taiko*-beats in the *music*. It is suggestive that the Court dancers did not presume to invent body movements in place of what had been forgotten, even though the Chūnagon Morokuzu accepted responsibility for shortening the music. This is in accordance with the observed conservatism of *dance* as opposed to the *music* for a given dance, to be observed in other cultures. Evidently the music of *Bugaku* was only of importance as a vehicle for the dance.

The grounds for shortening by *ten* drum-beat periods, even though the dancer had only forgotten eight periods of the dance, are indicated in Fascicle 1, p. 20, paragraph 4.

(9) In view of the alternative name of *Middle Prelude* for the *Stamping* of *Shunnō-den,* it is perhaps significant that this movement, and the measured portions of the *Middle Prelude* of *Toraden* are both in measures of $\frac{4}{2}$, in contrast to the *Entering Broaching* movements of both suites in measures of $\frac{3}{2}$.

(10) The following note on our transcriptions of ornaments in the zither and lute parts of JCYR and SGYR may be of assistance to those readers who wish to pursue further the composition of the original sources. Ornaments in zither parts, notated in tablature by a system of dots and hooks placed in specific positions on the main tablature sign, indicate changes of pitch by depressing, or depressing and releasing, or lowering tension, or lowering tension and releasing, the string with the left hand, after an initial single excitation of that string by the right hand. The gliding pitch-change resulting from this technique is represented in transcription by a line connecting the notes thus obtained. Ornaments in lute-parts, notated in the Japanese sources as one large tablature-sign followed by one, two, or (in exceptional cases) more, small tablature-signs,' written to the right of the main column of tablature-signs, are executed with a single right-hand plucking movement for the large tablature sign, and left-hand finger-plucking for the small tablature signs. Ideally, the plucked note in the *gruppetto* should be represented by a full-sized note, while the ornamental notes produced for both instruments by the left hand alone should be written as small notes. For convenience, however, all constituents of mordents and ligatures are written full-sized, and slurred to indicate their *gruppetto*-character. Detailed descriptions of types of ornamentation, and of the conventions adopted for representing these in staff-notation have been given in Wolpert 1979, pp. 443-9, Condit 1976, pp. 87-95 and (for both lute and zither) in Markham 1983, pp. 38-56 for lute and pp. 62-88 for zither.

Fascicle 4 will offer upwards of a dozen items from the second scroll of pieces belonging to the *Ichikotsu-chō* mode-key group, beginning with a first item overtly linked with Sogdiana, that Central Asian State which exerted so great an influence on the entertainment music of the Tang Court. The title of this piece shows clearly the roots of much of the *Tōgaku*-repertory in popular music: 'Sogdians drinking wine'.

Secondary sources

Akira Ishihara and Levy, Howard S. (1969) *The Tao of Sex: An Annotated Translation of the Twenty-eight Section of The Essence Of Medical Prescription* (Ishimpō), Yokohama: Shibundo

Birrell, Anne (1982) *New Songs from a Jade Terrace,* London

Coedes, G. (1948) *Les Etats hindouisés d'Indochine et d'Indonésie,* Paris

Condit, J. (1976) 'Differing transcriptions from the twelfth-century Japanese koto manuscript *Jinchi-yōroku*' *Ethnomusicology* XX, 1, pp. 87-95.

Demièville, P. (1925) 'La Musique Came au Japon', in *Publications de L'Ecole française d'extrême-orient: Etudes asiatiques publiées à l'occasion du vingt-cinquième anniversaire de l'Ecole française d'extrême-orient,* vol. 1, pp. 199-226

Eckardt, H., trans. (1956) *Das Kokonchomonshū des Tachibana Narisue als musikgeschichtliche Quelle,* Wiesbaden

Gimm, Martin (1966) *Das Yüeh-fu tsa-lu des Tuan An-chieh,* Wiesbaden

Gulik, R. H. van (1940) *The Lore of the Chinese Lute,* Tokyo
    (1961) *Sexual Life in Ancient China,* Leiden

Holzman, Donald (1957) *La Vie et la Penseê de Hi Kang,* Leiden

Karlgren,B. (1957) *Grammata Serica Recensa,* Stockholm

Kuttner, F. A. (1975) 'Prince Chu Tsai-yü's life and work – a re-evaluation of his contribution to equal temperament theory', *Ethnomusicology* XIX, pp. 163-206.

Marett, Allan J. (1976) 'Hakuga's flute score: a tenth-century Japanese source of "Tang-Music" in tablature', Ph.D. dissertation, 26 October, University Library, Cambridge, No. 9823
    (1977) 'Tunes notated in flute-tablature from a Japanese source of the tenth century', *Musica Asiatica* I, pp. 1-59

Markham, E. J. (1983) *Saibara – Japanese Court Songs of the Heian Period,* 2 vol, Cambridge

Picken, L. E. R. (1966) 'Secular Chinese songs of the twelfth century' *Studia Musicologica Academiae Scientarum Hungaricae,* vol. 8, pp. 125-72

    (1969) 'Tunes apt for T'ang lyrics from the *shō* 笙 part-books of *Tōgaku* 唐樂 ', in *Essays in Ethnomusicology...* a birthday offering for Lee Hye-ku, Seoul
    (1974) 'Tenri toshokan shozō no juyo na Togaku-fu ni kansuru oboegaki' *Biblia, 57,* pp. 2-12

Pulleyblank, E. G. (1960) 'Neo-Confucianism and Neo-Legalism in T'ang intellectual life, 755-805', in *The Confucian Persuasion,* ed. A. F. Wright, Stanford, Cal.

Schafer, E. H. (1963) *The Golden Peaches of Samarkand,* Berkeley and Los Angeles

Shiba Sukehiro (1972) *Gosen-fu ni yoru Gagaku-sōfu,* 五線譜による雅樂総譜 4 *maki* (vols), Tokyo

Soothill, W. E. and Hodous, L. (1937) *A Dictionary of Chinese Buddhist Terms,* London

Takakusu Junjirō(1929) 'Le Voyage de Kanshin en Orient (742-754), par Aomi-no Mabito Genkai (779)', in *Bulletin de l'Ecole française d'extrême-orient,* vol. 28, 1928, pp. 1-41
    (1930) *ibid.,* vol. 29, 1929, pp. 47-62

Vikár, László and Bereczki, Gábor (1971) *Cheremis Folksongs,* Budapest: Akadémiai Kiadó

Waley, Arthur (1938) *The Analects of Confucius,* London
    (1949) *The Life and Times of Po Chü-i,* London

Wolpert, Rembrandt (1977) 'A ninth-century lute tutor', *Musica Asiatica* 1, pp. 111-65
    (1979) 'The evolution of notated ornamentation in Tōgaku manuscripts for lute', *Sino-Mongolica, Festschrift für Herbert Franke, Münchener Ostasiatische Studien 25,* ed, W. Bauer, Wiesbaden

Wright, Arthur F., ed.(1960) *The Confucian Persuasion,* Stanford, Cal..
    (1978) *The Sui Dynasty,* New York

Yang ,YinLiu (1980) *Zhongguo gudai yinyue shigao* 中國古代音樂史稿 (A draft history of ancient Chinese music) Renmin yinyue chubanshe edn

12032210R00066

Printed in Great Britain
by Amazon.co.uk, Ltd.,
Marston Gate.